Pies & Pud~~dings~~

Publisher & Creative Director: Nick Wells
Senior Editor: Catherine Emslie
Designer: Vanessa Green
With thanks to: Gina Steer and Karen Fitzpatrick

This is a **FLAME TREE** Book

FLAME TREE PUBLISHING

Crabtree Hall, Crabtree Lane
Fulham, London SW6 6TY
United Kingdom
www.flametreepublishing.com

Flame Tree is part of The Foundry Creative Media Company Limited

First published 2007

08 10 11 09 07
1 3 5 7 9 10 8 6 4 2

ISBN-13 978 1 84451 726 8
ISBN-10 1 84451 726 8

A copy of the CIP data for this book is available from the British Library.

Printed in China

Pies & Puddings

Quick and Easy, Proven Recipes

**FLAME TREE
PUBLISHING**

Contents

Contents

Fish & Shellfish 98

Meat

Poultry

Contents

Vegetarian 266

Sweet Pies & Puddings 294

Hygiene in the Kitchen

It is well worth remembering that many foods can carry some form of bacteria. In most cases, the worst it will lead to is a bout of food poisoning or gastroenteritis, although for certain groups this can be more serious. The risk can be reduced or eliminated by good food hygiene and proper cooking.

Do not buy food that is past its sell-by date and do not consume any food that is past its use-by date. When buying food, use the eyes and nose. If the food looks tired, limp or a bad colour or it has a rank, acrid or simply bad smell, do not buy or eat it under any circumstances.

Regularly clean, defrost and clear out the refrigerator or freezer – it is worth checking the packaging to see exactly how long each product is safe to freeze.

Dish cloths and tea towels must be washed and changed regularly. Ideally use disposable cloths which should be replaced on a daily basis. More durable cloths should be left

to soak in bleach, then washed in the washing machine on a boil wash.

Always keep your hands, cooking utensils and food preparation surfaces clean and never allow pets to climb on to any work surfaces.

Buying

Avoid bulk buying where possible, especially fresh produce such as meat, poultry, fish, fruit and vegetables unless buying for the freezer. Fresh foods lose their nutritional value rapidly so buying a little at a time minimises loss of nutrients. It also eliminates a packed refrigerator which reduces the effectiveness of the refrigeration process.

When buying frozen foods, ensure that they are not heavily iced on the outside. Place in the freezer as soon as possible after purchase.

Preparation

Make sure that all work surfaces and utensils are clean and dry. Separate chopping boards should be used for raw and cooked meats, fish and vegetables. It is worth washing all fruits and vegetables regardless of whether they are going to be eaten raw or lightly cooked. Do not reheat food more than once.

All poultry must be thoroughly thawed before cooking. Leave the food in the refrigerator until it is completely thawed. Once defrosted, the chicken should be cooked as soon as possible. The only time food can be refrozen is when the food has been thoroughly thawed then cooked. Once the food has cooled then it can be frozen again for one month.

All poultry and game (except for duck) must be cooked thoroughly. When cooked the juices will run clear. Other

meats, like minced meat and pork should be cooked right the way through. Fish should turn opaque, be firm in texture and break easily into large flakes.

Storing, Refrigerating and Freezing

Meat, poultry, fish, seafood and dairy products should all be refrigerated. The temperature of the refrigerator should be between 1–5°C/34–41°F while the freezer temperature should not rise above -18°C/-0.4°F. When refrigerating cooked food, allow it to cool down quickly and completely before refrigerating. Hot food will raise the temperature of the refrigerator and possibly affect or spoil other food stored in it.

Food within the refrigerator and freezer should always be covered. Raw and cooked food should be stored in separate parts of the refrigerator. Cooked food should be kept on the top shelves of the refrigerator, while raw meat, poultry and fish should be placed on bottom shelves to avoid drips and cross-contamination.

High-Risk Foods

Certain foods may carry risks to people who are considered vulnerable such as the elderly, the ill, pregnant women, babies and those suffering from a recurring illness. It is advisable to avoid those foods which belong to a higher-risk category.

There is a slight chance that some eggs carry the bacteria salmonella. Cook the eggs until both the yolk and the white are firm to eliminate this risk. Sauces including Hollandaise, mayonnaise, mousses, soufflés and meringues all use raw or lightly cooked eggs, as do custard-based dishes, ice creams and sorbets. These are all considered high-risk foods to the vulnerable groups mentioned above. Certain meats and poultry also carry the potential risk of salmonella and so should be cooked thoroughly until the juices run clear and there is no pinkness left. Unpasteurised products such as milk, cheese (especially soft cheese), pâté, meat (both raw and cooked) all have the potential risk of listeria and should be avoided.

When buying seafood, buy from a reputable source. Fish should have bright clear eyes, shiny skin and bright pink or red gills. The fish should feel stiff to the touch, with a slight smell of sea air and iodine. The flesh of fish steaks and fillets should be translucent with no signs of discolouration. Avoid any molluscs that are open or do not close when tapped lightly. Univalves such as cockles or winkles should withdraw into their shells when lightly prodded. Squid and octopus should have firm flesh and a pleasant sea smell.

Care is required when freezing seafood. It is imperative to check whether the fish has been frozen before. If it has been, then it should not be frozen again under any circumstances.

Nutrition
The Role of Essential Nutrients

A healthy and well-balanced diet is the body's primary energy source. In children, it constitutes the building blocks for future health as well as providing lots of energy. In adults, it encourages self-healing and regeneration within the body. A well-balanced diet will provide the body with all the essential nutrients it needs. This can be achieved by eating a variety of foods, demonstrated in the pyramid below:

Fats
milk, yogurt
and cheese

Proteins
meat, fish, poultry, eggs,
nuts and pulses

*Fruits and
Vegetables*

Starchy Carbohydrates
cereals, potatoes, bread, rice and pasta

Fats

Fats fall into two categories: saturated and unsaturated fats. It is very important that a healthy balance is achieved within the diet. Fats are an essential part of the diet and a source of energy and provide essential fatty acids and fat soluble vitamins. The right balance of fats should boost the body's immunity to infection and keep muscles, nerves and arteries in good condition. Saturated fats are of animal origin and are hard when stored at room temperature. They can be found in dairy produce, meat, eggs, margarines and hard white cooking fat (lard) as well as in manufactured products such as pies, biscuits and cakes. A high intake of saturated fat over many years has been proven to increase heart disease and high blood cholesterol levels and often leads to weight gain. The aim of a healthy diet is to keep the fat content low in the foods that we eat. Lowering the amount of saturated fat that we consume is very important, but this does not mean that it is good to consume lots of other types of fat.

There are two kinds of unsaturated fats: polyunsaturated and monounsaturated. Polyunsaturated fats include the following oils: safflower oil, soybean oil, corn oil and sesame oil. Within the polyunsaturated group are Omega oils. The Omega-3 oils are of significant interest because they have been found to be particularly beneficial to coronary health and can encourage brain growth and development. They oils are derived from oily fish such as salmon, mackerel, herring, pilchards and sardines. It is recommended that we should eat these types of fish at least once a week. However, for those who do not eat fish, liver oil supplements are available in most supermarkers and health shops. It is suggested that these supplements should be taken on a daily basis. The most popular oils that are high in monounsaturates are olive oil, sunflower oil and peanut oil. The Mediterranean diet which is based on a diet high in monounsaturated fats is recommended for heart health. Also, monounsaturated fats are known to help reduce the levels of LDL (the bad) cholestrol. However, one type of unsaturated fat which should be avoided at all costs is 'trans fat'. This can be poly- or monounsaturated and is most commonly found in processed foods containing 'hydrogenated' oil or fat.

Proteins

Composed of amino acids, proteins perform a wide variety of essential functions for the body including supplying energy and building and repairing tissues. Good sources of proteins are eggs, milk, yogurt, cheese, meat, fish, poultry, eggs, nuts and pulses. (See the second level of the pyramid.) Some of these foods, however, contain saturated fats. To strike a nutritional balance eat generous amounts of vegetable protein foods such as soya, beans, lentils, peas and nuts.

Fruits and Vegetables

Not only are fruits and vegetables the most visually appealing foods, but they are extremely good for us, providing essential vitamins and minerals essential for growth, repair and protection in the human body. Fruits and vegetables are low in calories and are responsible for regulating the body's metabolic processes and controlling the composition of its fluids and cells.

Minerals

CALCIUM Important for healthy bones and teeth, nerve transmission, muscle contraction, blood clotting and hormone function. Calcium promotes a healthy heart, improves skin, relieves aching muscles and bones, maintains the correct acid-alkaline balance and reduces menstrual cramps. Good sources are dairy products, small bones of small fish, nuts, pulses, fortified white flours, breads and green leafy vegetables.

CHROMIUM Part of the glucose tolerance factor, chromium balances blood sugar levels, helps to normalise hunger and reduce cravings, improves lifespan, helps protect DNA and is essential for heart function. Good sources are brewer's yeast, wholemeal bread, rye bread, oysters, potatoes, green peppers, butter and parsnips.

IODINE Important for the manufacture of thyroid hormones and for normal development. Good sources of iodine are seafood, seaweed, milk and dairy products.

IRON As a component of haemoglobin, iron carries oxygen around the body. It is vital for normal growth and development. Good sources are liver, corned beef, red meat, fortified breakfast cereals, pulses, green leafy vegetables, egg yolk and cocoa and cocoa products.

MAGNESIUM Important for efficient functioning of metabolic enzymes and development of the skeleton. Magnesium promotes healthy muscles by helping them to relax and is therefore good for PMS. It is also important for heart muscles and the nervous system. Good sources are nuts, green vegetables, meat, cereals, milk and yogurt.

PHOSPHORUS Forms and maintains bones and teeth, builds muscle tissue, helps maintain pH of the body, aids metabolism and energy production. Phosphorus is present in almost all foods.

POTASSIUM Enables nutrients to move into cells, while waste products move out; promotes healthy nerves and muscles; maintains fluid balance in the body; helps secretion of insulin for blood sugar control to produce constant energy; relaxes muscles; maintains heart functioning and stimulates gut movement to encourage proper elimination. Good sources are fruit, vegetables, milk and bread.

SELENIUM Antioxidant properties help to protect against free radicals and carcinogens. Selenium reduces inflammation, stimulates the immune system to fight infections, promotes a healthy heart and helps vitamin E's action. It is also required for the male reproductive system and is needed for metabolism. Good sources are tuna, liver, kidney, meat, eggs, cereals, nuts and dairy products.

SODIUM Important in helping to control body fluid and balance, preventing dehydration. Sodium is involved in muscle and nerve function and helps move nutrients into cells. All foods are good sources; however, processed, pickled and salted foods can contain too much sodium.

ZINC Important for metabolism and the healing of wounds.

It also aids ability to cope with stress, promotes a healthy nervous system and brain especially in the growing foetus, aids bones and teeth formation and is essential for constant energy. Good sources are liver, meat, pulses, whole-grain cereals, nuts and oysters.

Vitamins

VITAMIN A Important for cell growth and developmemt and for the formation of visual pigments in the eye. Vitamin A comes in two forms: retinol and beta-carotenes. Retinol is found in liver, meat and meat products and whole milk and its products. Beta-carotene is a powerul antioxidant and is found in red and yellow fruits and vegetables such as carrots, mangoes and apricots.

VITAMIN B1 Important in releasing energy from carboydrate-containing foods. Good sources are yeast and yeast products, bread, fortified breakfast cereals and potatoes.

VITAMIN B2 Important for metabolism of proteins, fats and carbohydrates to produce energy. Good sources are meat, yeast extracts, fortified breakfast cereals and milk and its products.

VITAMIN B3 Required for metabolism of food into energy production. Good sources are milk and milk products, fortified breakfast cereals, pulses, meat, poultry and eggs.

VITAMIN B5 Important for metabolism of food and energy production. All foods are good sources but especially fortified breakfast cereals, whole-grain bread and dairy products.

VITAMIN B6 Important for metabolism of protein and fat. It may also be involved with the regulation of sex hormones. Good sources are liver, fish, pork, soya beans and peanuts.

VITAMIN B12 Important for the production of red blood cells and DNA. It is vital for growth and the nervous system. Good sources are meat, fish, eggs, poultry and milk.

BIOTIN Important for metabolism of fatty acids. Good sources of biotin are liver, kidney, eggs and nuts. Micro-organisms also manufacture this vitamin in the gut.

VITAMIN C Important for healing wounds and the formation of collagen which keeps skin and bones strong. It is an important antioxidant. Good sources are fruits, soft summer fruits and vegetables.

VITAMIN D Important for absorption and handling of calcium to help build bone strength. Good sources are oily fish, eggs, whole milk and milk products, margarine and, of course, sufficient exposure to sunlight, as vitamin D is made in the skin.

VITAMIN E Important as an antioxidant vitamin helping to protect cell membranes from damage. Good sources are vegetable oils, margarines, seeds, nuts and green vegetables.

FOLIC ACID Critical during pregnancy for the development of the brain and nerves. It is always essential for brain and nerve function and is needed for utilising protein and red blood cell formation. Good sources are whole-grain cereals, fortified breakfast cereals, green leafy vegetables, oranges and liver.

VITAMIN K Important for controlling blood clotting. Good sources are cauliflower, Brussels sprouts, lettuce, cabbage, beans, broccoli, peas, asparagus, potatoes, corn oil, tomatoes and milk.

Carbohydrates

Carbohydrates are an energy source and come in two forms: starch and sugar. Starch carbohydrates are also known as complex carbohydrates and they include all cereals, potatoes, breads, rice and pasta. (See the fourth level of the pyramid). Eating wholegrain varieties of these foods also provides fibre. Diets high in fibre are believed to be beneficial in helping to prevent bowel cancer and can also keep cholesterol down. High-fibre diets are also good for those concerned about weight gain. Fibre is bulky and fills the stomach, therefore reducing hunger pangs. Sugar carbohydrates, which are also known as fast-release carbohydrates because of the quick fix of energy they give to the body, include sugar and sugar-sweetened products such as jams and syrups. Milk provides lactose which is a milk sugar and fruits provide fructose which is a fruit sugar.

Basic Baking Techniques

There is no mystery to successful baking, it really is easy providing you follow a few simple rules and guidelines. First, read the recipe right through before commencing. There is nothing more annoying than getting to the middle of a recipe and discovering that you are minus one or two of the ingredients. Until you are confident, follow a recipe, do not try a short cut otherwise you may find that you have left out a vital step which means that the recipe really cannot work. Most of all, have patience, baking is easy – if you can read, you can bake.

Pastry Making

Pastry needs to be kept as cool as possible through-out. Cool hands help, but are not essential. Use cold or iced water, but not too much as pastry does not need to be wet. Make sure that your fat is not runny or melted but firm (this is why block fat is the best). Avoid using too much flour when rolling out as this alters the proportions and also avoid handling the dough too much. Roll in one direction as this helps to ensure that

Hints for successful baking

Ensure that the ingredients are accurately measured. A cake that has too much flour or insufficient egg will be dry and crumbly. Take care when measuring the raising agent if used, as too much will mean that the cake will rise too quickly and then sink. Insufficient raising agent means the cake will not rise in the first place.

Ensure that the oven is preheated to the correct temperature, it can take 10 minutes to reach 180˚C/350˚F/Gas Mark 4. You may find that an oven thermometer is a good investment. Cakes are best if cooked in the centre of the preheated oven. Try to avoid opening the oven door at the start of cooking as a draft can make the cake sink. If using a fan oven refer to the manufacturers' instructions.

Check that the cake is thoroughly cooked by removing from the oven and inserting a clean skewer. Leave for 30 seconds and remove. If clean then the cake is cooked, if there is a little mixture return to the oven for a few minutes.

Other problems while cake making are insufficient creaming of the fat and sugar or a curdled creamed mixture (which will result in a fairly solid cake). Flour that has not been folded in carefully enough or has not been mixed with enough raising agent may also result in a fairly heavy consistency. Ensure that the correct size of tin is used as you may end up either with a flat, hard cake or one which has spilled over the edge of the tin. Be aware – especially when cooking with fruit – that if the consistency is too soft, the cake will not be able to support the fruit.

Finally, when you take your cake out of the oven, unless the recipe states that it should be left in the tin until cold, leave for a few minutes, then loosen the edges and turn out on to a wire rack to cool. Cakes which are left in the tin for too long, tend to sink or slightly overcook. When storing, make sure the cake is completely cold before placing it into an airtight tin or plastic container.

the pastry does not shrink. Allow the pastry to rest, preferably in the refrigerator after rolling. If you follow these guidelines but your pastry is still not as good as you would like it to be, then make it in a food processor instead.

Lining a Flan Case

It is important to choose the right tin to bake with. You will often find that a loose-bottomed metal flan case is the best option as it conducts heat more efficiently and evenly than a ceramic dish. It also has the advantage of a removable base which makes transferring the final flan easy; it simply lifts out keeping the pastry intact.

Roll the pastry out on a lightly floured surface ensuring that it is a few inches larger than the flan case. Wrap the pastry round the rolling pin, lift and place in the tin. Carefully ease the pastry into the base and sides of the tin, ensuring that there are no tears in the pastry. Allow to rest for a few minutes then trim the edge either with a sharp knife or by rolling a rolling pin across the top of the flan tin.

Baking Blind

The term baking blind means that the pastry case needs to be cooked without the filling, resulting in a crisp pastry shell that is either partially or fully cooked depending on whether the filling needs any cooking. Pastry shells can be prepared ahead of time as they last for several days if stored correctly in an airtight container or longer if frozen.

To bake blind, line a pastry case with the prepared pastry and allow to rest in the refrigerator for 30 minutes. This will help

to minimize shrinkage while it is being cooked. Remove from the refrigerator and lightly prick the base all over with a fork (do not do this if the filling is runny). Brush with a little beaten egg if desired or simply line the case with a large square of greaseproof paper, big enough to cover both the base and sides of the pastry case. Fill with either ceramic baking beans or dried beans. Place on a baking sheet and bake in a preheated oven, generally at 200°C/400°F/Gas Mark 6, remembering that ovens can take at least 15 minutes to reach this heat. Cook for 10–12 minutes, then remove from the oven, discard the paper and beans. Return to the oven and continue to cook for a further 5–10 minutes depending on whether the filling needs cooking. Normally, unless otherwise stated, individual pastry tartlet cases also benefit from baking blind.

Covering a Pie Dish

To cover a pie, roll out the pastry until it is about two inches larger than the circumference of the dish. Cut a 2.5 cm/ 1 inch strip from around the outside of the pastry and then moisten the edge of the pie dish you are using. Place the strip on the edge of the dish and brush with water or beaten egg. Generously fill the pie dish until the surface is slightly rounded. Using the rolling pin, lift the remaining pastry and cover the pie dish. Press together, then seal. Using a sharp knife, trim off any excess pastry from around the edges. Try to avoid brushing the edges of the pastry especially puff pastry as this prevents the pastry rising evenly. Before placing in the oven make a small hole in the centre of the pie to allow the steam to escape.

The edges of the pie can be forked by pressing the back of a fork around the edge of the pie or instead crimp by pinching the edge crust holding the thumb and index finger of your right hand against the edge while gently pushing with the index finger of your left hand. Other ways of finishing the pie are to knock up (achieved by gently pressing your index finger down

on to the rim and, at the same time, tapping a knife horizontally along the edge giving it a flaky appearance), or fluting the edges by pressing your thumb down on the edge of the pastry while gently drawing back an all-purpose knife about 1 cm/½ inch and repeating around the rim. Experiment by putting leaves and berries made out of leftover pastry to finish off the pie, then brush the top of the pie with beaten egg.

Lining Cake Tins

If a recipe states that the tin needs lining do not be tempted to ignore this. Rich fruit cakes and other cakes that take a long time to cook benefit from the tin being lined so that the edges and base do not burn or dry out. Greaseproof or baking parchment paper is ideal for this. It is a good idea to have the paper at least double thickness, or preferably 3–4 thicknesses. Sponge cakes and other cakes that are cooked in 30 minutes or less are also better if the bases are lined as it is far easier to remove them from the tin.

The best way to line a round or square tin is to lightly draw around the base and then cut just inside the markings making it easy to sit in the tin. Next, lightly oil the paper so it easily peels away from the cake. If the sides of the tin also need to be lined, then cut a strip of paper long enough for the tin. This can be measured by wrapping a piece of string around the rim of the tin. Once again, lightly oil the paper, push against the tin and oil once more as this will hold the paper to the sides of the tin. Steamed puddings usually need only a disc of greaseproof paper at the bottom of the dish as the sides come away easily.

Appetizers

Sticky Braised Spare Ribs

SERVES 4

900 g/2 lb meaty pork spare ribs, cut crossways into 7.5 cm/3 inch pieces
125 ml/4 fl oz apricot nectar or orange juice
50 ml/2 fl oz dry white wine
3 tbsp black bean sauce

3 tbsp tomato ketchup
2 tbsp clear honey
3–4 spring onions, trimmed and chopped
2 garlic cloves, peeled and crushed
grated zest of 1 small orange

salt and freshly ground black pepper

To garnish:
spring onion tassels
lemon wedges

Put the spare ribs in the wok and add enough cold water to cover. Bring to the boil over a medium-high heat, skimming any scum that rises to the surface. Cover and simmer for 30 minutes, then drain and rinse the ribs.

Rinse and dry the wok and return the ribs to it. In a bowl, blend the apricot nectar or orange juice with the white wine, black bean sauce, tomato ketchup and the honey until smooth.

Stir in the spring onions, garlic cloves and grated orange zest. Stir well until mixed thoroughly.

Pour the mixture over the spare ribs in the wok and stir gently until the ribs are lightly coated. Place over a moderate heat and bring to the boil.

Cover then simmer, stirring occasionally, for 1 hour, or until the ribs are tender and the sauce is thickened and sticky. (If the sauce reduces too quickly or begins to stick, add water 1 tablespoon at a time until the ribs are tender.) Adjust the seasoning to taste, then transfer the ribs to a serving plate and garnish with spring onion tassels and lemon wedges. Serve immediately.

Try This: FOR A MAIN MEAL: 110   FOR PUDDING: 318

Swedish Cocktail Meatballs

SERVES 4–6

50 g/2 oz butter
1 onion, peeled and finely
  chopped
50 g/2 oz fresh white
  breadcrumbs
1 medium egg, beaten

125 ml/4 fl oz double cream
salt and freshly ground
  black pepper
350 g/12 oz fresh lean
  beef mince
125 g/4 oz fresh pork mince

3–4 tbsp freshly chopped dill
½ tsp ground allspice
1 tbsp vegetable oil
125 ml/4 fl oz beef stock
cream cheese and chive or
  cranberry sauce, to serve

Heat half the butter in a large wok, add the onion and cook, stirring frequently, for 4–6 minutes, or until softened and beginning to colour. Transfer to a bowl and leave to cool. Wipe out the wok with absorbent kitchen paper.

Add the breadcrumbs and beaten egg with 1–2 tablespoons of cream to the softened onion. Season to taste with salt and pepper and stir until well blended. Using your fingertips crumble the beef and pork mince into the bowl. Add half the dill, the allspice and, using your hands, mix together until well blended. With dampened hands, shape the mixture into 2.5 cm/1 inch balls.

Melt the remaining butter in the wok and add the vegetable oil, swirling it to coat the side of the wok. Working in batches, add about one quarter to one third of the meatballs in a single layer and cook for 5 minutes, swirling and turning until golden and cooked.

Transfer to a plate and continue with the remaining meatballs, transferring them to the plate as they are cooked. Pour off the fat in the wok. Add the beef stock and bring to the boil, then boil until reduced by half, stirring and scraping up any browned bits from the bottom. Add the remaining cream and continue to simmer until slightly thickened and reduced.

Stir in the remaining dill and season if necessary. Add the meatballs and simmer for 2–3 minutes, or until heated right through. Serve with cocktail sticks, with the sauce for dipping.

Try This: FOR A MAIN MEAL: 138   FOR PUDDING: 298

Fried Pork–filled Wontons

MAKES 24

For the filling:
275 g/10 oz cooked pork, finely chopped
2–3 spring onions, trimmed and finely chopped
2.5 cm/1 inch piece fresh root ginger, grated
1 garlic clove, peeled and crushed
1 small egg, lightly beaten
1 tbsp soy sauce

1 tsp soft light brown sugar
1 tsp sweet chilli sauce or tomato ketchup

24–30 wonton wrappers, 8 cm/3½ inches square
300 ml/½ pint vegetable oil for deep frying

For the ginger dipping sauce
4 tbsp soy sauce

1–2 tbsp rice or raspberry vinegar
2.5 cm/1 inch piece fresh root ginger, peeled and finely slivered
1 tbsp sesame oil
1 tbsp soft light brown sugar
2–3 dashes hot chilli sauce
spring onion tassels, to garnish

Place all the filling ingredients into a food processor and, using the pulse button, process until well blended. Do not overwork, the filling should have a coarse texture.

Lay out the wonton wrappers on a clean chopping board and put a teaspoon of the filling in the centre of each. Brush the edges with a little water and bring up 2 opposite corners of each square over the filling to form a triangle, pressing the edges firmly to seal. Dampen the 2 other corners and overlap them slightly, pressing firmly to seal, to form an open-envelope shape, similar to a tortellini.

For the dipping sauce, stir together all the ingredients until the sugar is dissolved. Pour into a serving bowl and reserve.

Heat the oil in a large wok to 190°C/375°F, or until a small cube of bread browns in about 30 seconds. Working in batches of 5–6, fry until the wontons are crisp and golden, turning once or twice. Remove and drain on absorbent kitchen paper. Garnish with spring onion tassels and serve hot with the dipping sauce.

Try This: FOR A MAIN MEAL: 246   FOR PUDDING: 316

Bacon, Mushroom & Cheese Puffs

SERVES 4

1 tbsp olive oil
225 g/8 oz field mushrooms, wiped and roughly chopped
225 g/8 oz rindless streaky bacon, roughly chopped

2 tbsp freshly chopped parsley
salt and freshly ground black pepper
350 g/12 oz ready-rolled puff pastry sheets, thawed if frozen

25 g/1 oz Emmenthal, or Cheddar cheese, grated
1 medium egg, beaten
salad leaves such as rocket or watercress, to garnish
tomatoes, to serve

Preheat the oven to 200°C/400°F/Gas Mark 6. Heat the olive oil in a large frying pan.

Add the mushrooms and bacon and fry for 6–8 minutes until golden in colour. Stir in the parsley, season to taste with salt and pepper and allow to cool.

Roll the sheet of pastry a little thinner on a lightly floured surface to a 30.5 cm/12 inch square. Cut the pastry into 4 equal squares.

Stir the grated cheese into the mushroom mixture. Spoon a quarter of the mixture on to one half of each square. Brush the edges of the square with a little of the beaten egg. Fold over the pastry to form a triangular parcel. Seal the edges well and place on a lightly oiled baking sheet. Repeat until the squares are done.

Make shallow slashes in the top of the pastry with a knife. Brush the parcels with the remaining beaten egg and cook in the preheated oven for 20 minutes, or until puffy and golden brown.

Serve warm or cold, garnished with the salad leaves and served with tomatoes.

Try This: FOR A MAIN MEAL: 112   FOR PUDDING: 298

Chicken–filled Spring Rolls

MAKES 12–14 ROLLS

For the filling:
1 tbsp vegetable oil
2 slices streaky bacon, diced
225 g/8 oz skinless chicken
 breast fillets, thinly sliced
1 small red pepper,
 deseeded and finely
 chopped
4 spring onions, trimmed
 and finely chopped

2.5 cm/1 inch piece fresh
 root ginger, peeled and
 finely chopped
75 g/3 oz mangetout peas,
 thinly sliced
75 g/3 oz beansprouts
1 tbsp soy sauce
2 tsp Chinese rice wine or
 dry sherry
2 tsp hoisin or plum sauce

For the wrappers:
3 tbsp plain flour
12–14 spring roll wrappers
300 ml/½ pint vegetable oil
 for deep frying
shredded spring onions, to
 garnish
dipping sauce, to serve

Heat a large wok, add the oil and when hot add the diced bacon and stir-fry for 2–3 minutes, or until golden. Add the chicken and pepper and stir-fry for a further 2–3 minutes. Add the remaining filling ingredients and stir-fry 3–4 minutes until all the vegetables are tender. Turn into a colander and leave to drain as the mixture cools completely.

Blend the flour with about 1½ tablespoons of water to form a paste. Soften each wrapper in a plate of warm water for 1–2 seconds, then place on a chopping board. Put 2–3 tablespoons of filling on the near edge. Fold the edge over the filling to cover. Fold in each side and roll up. Seal the edge with a little flour paste and press to seal securely. Transfer to a baking sheet, seam-side down.

Heat the oil in a large wok to 190°C/375°F, or until a small cube of bread browns in about 30 seconds. Working in batches of 3–4, fry the spring rolls until they are crisp and golden, turning once (about 2 minutes). Remove and drain on absorbent kitchen paper. Arrange the spring rolls on a serving plate, garnish with spring onion tassels and serve hot with dipping sauce.

Try This: FOR A MAIN MEAL: 174 FOR PUDDING: 314

Crostini with Chicken Livers

SERVES 4

2 tbsp olive oil
2 tbsp butter
1 shallot, peeled and finely
    chopped
1 garlic clove, peeled and
    crushed
150 g/5 oz chicken livers

1 tbsp plain flour
2 tbsp dry white wine
1 tbsp brandy
50 g/2 oz mushrooms, sliced
salt and freshly ground black
    pepper
4 slices of ciabatta

To garnish:
fresh sage leaves
lemon wedges

Heat 1 tablespoon of the olive oil and 1 tablespoon of the butter in a frying pan, add the shallot and garlic and cook gently for 2–3 minutes.

Trim and wash the chicken livers thoroughly and pat dry on absorbent kitchen paper as much as possible. Cut into slices, then toss in the flour. Add the livers to the frying pan with the shallot and garlic and continue to fry for a further 2 minutes, stirring continuously.

Pour in the white wine and brandy and bring to the boil. Boil rapidly for 1–2 minutes to allow the alcohol to evaporate, then stir in the sliced mushrooms and cook gently for about 5 minutes, or until the chicken livers are cooked, but just a little pink inside. Season to taste with salt and pepper.

Fry the slices of ciabatta or similar-style bread in the remaining oil and butter, then place on individual serving dishes. Spoon over the liver mixture and garnish with a few sage leaves and lemon wedges. Serve immediately.

Try This: FOR A MAIN MEAL: 116   FOR PUDDING: 320

Smoked Mackerel Vol–au–Vents

SERVES 1–2

350 g/12 oz prepared puff pastry
1 small egg, beaten
2 tsp sesame seeds
225 g/8 oz peppered smoked

mackerel, skinned and chopped
5 cm/2 inch piece cucumber
4 tbsp soft cream cheese
2 tbsp cranberry sauce

1 tbsp freshly chopped dill
1 tbsp finely grated lemon rind
dill sprigs, to garnish
mixed salad leaves, to serve

Preheat the oven to 230°C/450°F/Gas Mark 8. Roll the pastry out on a lightly floured surface and using a 9 cm/3½ inch fluted cutter cut out 12 rounds. Using a 1 cm/½ inch cutter mark a lid in the centre of each round.

Place on a damp baking sheet and brush the rounds with a little beaten egg. Sprinkle the pastry with the sesame seeds and bake in the preheated oven for 10–12 minutes, or until golden brown and well risen.

Transfer the vol-au-vents to a chopping board and when cool enough to touch carefully remove the lids with a small sharp knife. Scoop out any uncooked pastry from the inside of each vol-au-vent, then return to the oven for 5–8 minutes to dry out. Remove and allow to cool.

Flake the mackerel into small pieces and reserve. Peel the cucumber if desired, cut into very small dice and add to the mackerel.

Beat the soft cream cheese with the cranberry sauce, dill and lemon rind. Stir in the mackerel and cucumber and use to fill the vol-au-vents. Place the lids on top, garnish with dill sprigs and serve with mixed salad leaves.

Try This: FOR A MAIN MEAL: 188   FOR PUDDING: 322

Prawn Toasts

SERVES 8–10

225 g/8 oz cooked peeled prawns, thawed if frozen, well drained and dried
1 medium egg white
2 spring onions, trimmed and chopped
1 cm/1½ inch piece fresh root ginger, peeled

and chopped
1 garlic clove, peeled and chopped
1 tsp cornflour
2–3 dashes hot pepper sauce
½ tsp sugar
salt and freshly ground black pepper

8 slices firm-textured white bread
4–5 tbsp sesame seeds
300 ml/½ pint vegetable oil for deep frying
sprigs of fresh coriander, to garnish

Put the prawns, egg white, spring onions, ginger, garlic, cornflour, hot pepper sauce and sugar into a food processor. Season to taste with about ½ teaspoon of salt and black pepper. Process until the mixture forms a smooth paste, scraping down the side of the bowl once or twice.

Using a metal palette knife, spread an even layer of the paste evenly over the bread slices. Sprinkle each slice generously with sesame seeds, pressing gently to bury them in the paste.

Trim the crusts off each slice, then cut each slice diagonally into 4 triangles. Cut each triangle in half again to make 8 pieces from each slice.

Heat the vegetable oil in a large wok to 190°C/375°F, or until a small cube of bread browns in about 30 seconds. Working in batches, fry the prawn triangles for 30–60 seconds, or until they are golden, turning once. Remove with a slotted spoon and drain on absorbent kitchen paper. Keep the toasts warm. Arrange them on a large serving plate and garnish with sprigs of fresh coriander. Serve immediately.

Try This: FOR A MAIN MEAL: 174 FOR PUDDING: 358

Potato Pancakes

SERVES 6

For the sauce:
4 tbsp crème fraîche
1 tbsp horseradish sauce
grated rind and juice of 1 lime
1 tbsp freshly snipped chives

For the pancakes:
225 g/8 oz floury potatoes,
   peeled and cut into chunks
1 small egg white
2 tbsp milk
2 tsp self-raising flour
1 tbsp freshly chopped thyme

large pinch of salt
a little vegetable oil,
   for frying
225 g/8 oz smoked mackerel
   fillets, skinned
fresh herbs, to garnish

To make the sauce, mix together the crème fraîche, horseradish, lime rind and juice and chives. Cover and reserve.

Place the potatoes in a large saucepan and cover with lightly salted boiling water. Bring back to the boil, cover and simmer for 15 minutes, or until the potatoes are tender. Drain and mash until smooth. Cool for 5 minutes, then whisk in the egg white, milk, flour, thyme and salt to form a thick smooth batter. Leave to stand for 30 minutes, then stir before using.

Heat a little oil in a heavy-based frying pan. Add 2–3 large spoonfuls of batter to make a small pancake and cook for 1–2 minutes until golden. Flip the pancake and cook for a further minute, or until golden. Repeat with the remaining batter to make 8 pancakes.

Arrange the pancakes on a plate and top with the smoked mackerel. Garnish with herbs and serve immediately with spoonfuls of the reserved horseradish sauce.

Try This: FOR A MAIN MEAL: 176   FOR PUDDING: 332

Potato Skins

SERVES 4

4 large baking potatoes
2 tbsp olive oil
2 tsp paprika
125 g/4 oz pancetta, roughly
   chopped

6 tbsp double cream
125 g/4 oz Gorgonzola
   cheese
1 tbsp freshly chopped
   parsley

To serve:
mayonnaise
sweet chilli dipping sauce
tossed green salad

Preheat the oven to 200˚C/400˚F/Gas Mark 6. Scrub the potatoes, then prick a few times with a fork or skewer and place directly on the top shelf of the oven. Bake in the preheated oven for at least 1 hour, or until tender. The potatoes are cooked when they yield gently to the pressure of your hand.

Set the potatoes aside until cool enough to handle, then cut in half and scoop the flesh into a bowl and reserve. Preheat the grill and line the grill rack with tinfoil.

Mix together the oil and the paprika and use half to brush the outside of the potato skins. Place on the grill rack under the preheated hot grill and cook for 5 minutes, or until crisp, turning as necessary.

Heat the remaining paprika-flavoured oil and gently fry the pancetta until crisp. Add to the potato flesh along with the cream, Gorgonzola cheese and parsley. Halve the potato skins and fill with the Gorgonzola filling. Return to the oven for a further 15 minutes to heat through. Sprinkle with a little more paprika and serve immediately with mayonnaise, sweet chilli sauce and a green salad.

Try This: FOR A MAIN MEAL: 158   FOR PUDDING: 354

Sweetcorn Fritters

SERVES 4

3 tbsp groundnut oil
1 small onion, peeled and
    finely chopped
1 red chilli, deseeded and
    finely chopped
1 garlic clove, peeled

and crushed
1 tsp ground coriander
325 g can sweetcorn
6 spring onions, trimmed
    and finely sliced
1 medium egg, lightly beaten

salt and freshly ground black
    pepper
3 tbsp plain flour
1 tsp baking powder
spring onion curls, to garnish
Thai-style chutney, to serve

Heat 1 tablespoon of the groundnut oil in a frying pan, add the onion and cook gently for 7–8 minutes or until beginning to soften. Add the chilli, garlic and ground coriander and cook for 1 minute, stirring continuously. Remove from the heat.

Drain the sweetcorn and tip into a mixing bowl. Lightly mash with a potato masher to break down the corn a little. Add the cooked onion mixture to the bowl with the spring onions and beaten egg. Season to taste with salt and pepper, then stir to mix together. Sift the flour and baking powder over the mixture and stir in.

Heat 2 tablespoons of the groundnut oil in a large frying pan. Drop 4 or 5 heaped teaspoonfuls of the sweetcorn mixture into the pan, and using a fish slice or spatula, flatten each to make a 1 cm/½ inch thick fritter.

Fry the fritters for 3 minutes, or until golden brown on the underside, turn over and fry for a further 3 minutes, or until cooked through and crisp.

Remove the fritters from the pan and drain on absorbent kitchen paper. Keep warm while cooking the remaining fritters, adding a little more oil if needed. Garnish with spring onion curls and serve immediately with a Thai-style chutney.

Try This: FOR A MAIN MEAL: 134   FOR PUDDING: 324

French Onion Tart

SERVES 4

For the quick flaky pastry:
125 g/4 oz butter
175 g/6 oz plain flour
pinch of salt

For the filling:
2 tbsp olive oil
4 large onions, peeled and
  thinly sliced
3 tbsp white wine vinegar
2 tbsp muscovado sugar

175 g/6 oz Cheddar
  cheese, grated
a little beaten egg or milk
salt and freshly ground
  black pepper

Preheat the oven to 200°C/400°F/Gas Mark 6. Place the butter in the freezer for 30 minutes. Sift the flour and salt into a large bowl. Grate the butter using the coarse side of a grater, dipping the butter in the flour every now and again as it makes it easier to grate.

Mix the butter into the flour, using a knife, making sure all the butter is coated thoroughly with flour. Add 2 tablespoons of cold water and continue to mix, bringing the mixture together. Use your hands to complete the mixing. Add a little more water if needed to leave a clean bowl. Place the pastry in a polythene bag and chill in the refrigerator for 30 minutes.

Heat the oil in a large frying pan, then fry the onions for 10 minutes, stirring occasionally until softened. Stir in the white wine vinegar and sugar. Increase the heat and stir frequently for another 4–5 minutes until the onions turn a deep caramel colour. Cook for another 5 minutes, then reserve to cool.

On a lightly floured surface, roll out the pastry to a 35.5 cm/14 inch circle. Wrap over a rolling pin and move the circle on to a baking sheet. Sprinkle half the cheese over the pastry, leaving a 5 cm/2 inch border around the edge, then spoon the caramelised onions over the cheese. Fold the uncovered pastry edges over the edge of the filling to form a rim and brush the rim with beaten egg or milk. Season to taste with salt and pepper. Sprinkle over the remaining Cheddar and bake for 20–25 minutes. Transfer to a large plate and serve immediately.

Try This: FOR A MAIN MEAL: 234 FOR PUDDING: 346

Mozzarella Parcels with Cranberry Relish

SERVES 6

125 g/4 oz mozzarella cheese
8 slices of thin white bread
2 medium eggs, beaten
salt and freshly ground black
   pepper

300 ml/½ pint olive oil

For the relish:
125 g/4 oz cranberries
2 tbsp fresh orange juice

grated rind of 1 small orange
50 g/2 oz soft light brown
   sugar
1 tbsp port

Slice the mozzarella thinly, remove the crusts from the bread and make sandwiches with the bread and cheese. Cut into 5 cm/2 inch squares and squash them quite flat. Season the eggs with salt and pepper, then soak the bread in the seasoned egg for 1 minute on each side until well coated.

Heat the oil to 190°C/375°F and deep-fry the bread squares for 1–2 minutes, or until they are crisp and golden brown. Drain on absorbent kitchen paper and keep warm while the cranberry relish is prepared.

Place the cranberries, orange juice, rind, sugar and port into a small saucepan and add 5 tablespoons of water. Bring to the boil, then simmer for 10 minutes, or until the cranberries have 'popped'. Sweeten with a little more sugar if necessary.

Arrange the mozzarella parcels on individual serving plates. Serve with a little of the cranberry relish.

Try This: FOR A MAIN MEAL: 190   FOR PUDDING: 320

Olive & Feta Parcels

MAKES 30

1 small red pepper	black olives	6 sheets filo pastry
1 small yellow pepper	125 g/4 oz feta cheese	3 tbsp olive oil
125 g/4 oz assorted	2 tbsp pine nuts, lightly	sour cream and chive dip,
marinated green and	toasted	to serve

Preheat the oven to 180°C/350°F/Gas Mark 4. Preheat the grill, then line the grill rack with tinfoil.

Cut the peppers into quarters and remove the seeds. Place skin side up on the foil-lined grill rack and cook under the preheated grill for 10 minutes, turning occasionally until the skins begin to blacken.

Place the peppers in a polythene bag and leave until cool enough to handle, then skin and thinly slice. Chop the olives and cut the feta cheese into small cubes. Mix together the olives, feta, sliced peppers and pine nuts.

Cut 1 sheet of filo pastry in half then brush with a little of the oil. Place a spoonful of the olive and feta mix about one-third of the way up the pastry.

Fold over the pastry and wrap to form a square parcel encasing the filling completely. Place this parcel in the centre of the second half of the pastry sheet. Brush the edges lightly with a little oil, bring up the corners to meet in the centre and twist them loosely to form a purse. Brush with a little more oil and repeat with the remaining filo pastry and filling.

Place the parcels on a lightly oiled baking sheet and bake in the preheated oven for 10–15 minutes, or until crisp and golden brown. Serve with the dip.

Try This: FOR A MAIN MEAL: 186   FOR PUDDING: 352

Hot Herby Mushrooms

SERVES 4

4 thin slices of white bread, crusts removed
125 g/4 oz chestnut mushrooms, wiped and sliced
125 g/4 oz oyster

mushrooms, wiped
1 garlic clove, peeled and crushed
1 tsp Dijon mustard
300 ml/½ pint chicken stock
salt and freshly ground

black pepper
1 tbsp freshly chopped parsley
1 tbsp freshly snipped chives, plus extra to garnish
mixed salad leaves to serve

Preheat the oven to 180°C/350°F/Gas Mark 4. With a rolling pin, roll each piece of bread out as thinly as possible. Press each piece of bread into a 10 cm/4 inch tartlet tin. Push each piece firmly down, then bake in the preheated oven for 20 minutes.

Place the mushrooms in a frying pan with the garlic, mustard and chicken stock and stir-fry over a moderate heat until the mushrooms are tender and the liquid is reduced by half.

Carefully remove the mushrooms from the frying pan with a slotted spoon and transfer to a heat-resistant dish. Cover with tinfoil and place in the bottom of the oven to keep the mushrooms warm.

Boil the remaining pan juices until reduced to a thick sauce. Season with salt and pepper.

Stir the parsley and the chives into the mushroom mixture.

Place one bread tartlet case on each plate and divide the mushroom mixture between them. Spoon over the pan juices, garnish with the chives and serve immediately with mixed salad leaves.

Try This: FOR A MAIN MEAL: 222   FOR PUDDING: 344

Wild Garlic Mushrooms with Pizza Breadsticks

SERVES 6

For the breadsticks:
7 g/¼ oz dried yeast
250 ml/8 fl oz warm water
400 g/14 oz strong,
  plain flour
2–3 tbsp olive oil
1 tsp salt, plus extra to sprinkle
1 red pepper, deseeded

50 g/2 oz grated
  cheddar cheese

For the mushrooms:
6 tbsp olive oil
4 garlic cloves, peeled
  and crushed
450 g/1 lb mixed wild

mushrooms, wiped
  and dried
salt and freshly ground
  black pepper
1 tbsp freshly chopped parsley
1 tbsp freshly chopped basil
1 tsp fresh oregano leaves
juice of 1 lemon

Preheat oven to 240°C/475°F/Gas Mark 9, 15 minutes before baking. Place the dried yeast in the warm water for 10 minutes. Place the flour in a large bowl and gradually blend in 1 tablespoon of the olive oil, the teaspoon of salt and the dissolved yeast.

Knead on a lightly floured surface to form a smooth and pliable dough. Cover with clingfilm and leave in a warm place for 15 minutes to allow the dough to rise, then roll out again and cut into sticks of equal length. Cover and leave to rise again for 10 minutes. Brush with 1–2 tablespoons of olive oil. Cut the pepper into thin strips and arrange on top of the dough. Sprinkle over the cheese and a little salt, and bake in the preheated oven for 10 minutes.

Meanwhile pour 2 tablespoons of the oil into a frying pan and add the crushed garlic. Cook over a very low heat, stirring well for 3–4 minutes to flavour the oil. Cut the wild mushrooms into bite-sized slices if very large, then add to the pan. Season well with salt and pepper and cook very gently for 6–8 minutes, or until tender.

Whisk the fresh herbs, the remaining olive oil and lemon juice together. Pour over the mushrooms and heat through. Season to taste and place on individual serving dishes. Serve with the pizza breadsticks.

Try This: FOR A MAIN MEAL: 208 FOR PUDDING: 372

Savoury Pies & Pastry

Cornish Pasties

MAKES 8

For the pastry:
350 g/12 oz self-raising flour
75 g/3 oz butter or margarine
75 g/3 oz lard or white
    vegetable fat
salt and freshly ground black
    pepper

For the filling:
550 g/1¼ lb braising steak,
    chopped very finely
1 large onion, peeled and
    finely chopped
1 large potato, peeled and
    diced
200 g/7 oz swede, peeled

and diced
3 tbsp Worcestershire sauce
salt and freshly ground black
    pepper
1 small egg, beaten, to glaze
cherry tomatoes, to serve
sprigs of fresh parsley, to
    garnish

Preheat the oven to 180°C/350°F/Gas Mark 4, about 15 minutes before required. To make the pastry, sift the flour into a large bowl and add the fats, chopped into little pieces. Rub the fats and flour together until the mixture resembles coarse breadcrumbs. Season to taste with salt and pepper and mix again. Add about 2 tablespoons of cold water, a little at a time, and mix until the mixture comes together to form a firm but pliable dough. Turn onto a lightly floured surface, knead until smooth, then wrap and chill in the refrigerator.

To make the filling, put the braising steak in a large bowl with the onion. Add the potatoes and swede to the bowl together with the Worcestershire sauce and salt and pepper. Mix well.

Divide the dough into 8 balls and roll each ball into a circle about 25.5 cm/10 inches across. Divide the filling between the circles of pastry. Wet the edge of the pastry, then fold over the filling. Pinch the edges to seal. Transfer the pasties to a lightly oiled baking sheet. Make a couple of small holes in each pasty and brush with beaten egg. Cook in the preheated oven for 15 minutes, remove and brush again with the egg. Return to the oven for a further 15–20 minutes until golden. Cool slightly, garnish with parsley and serve with cherry tomatoes.

Try This: FOR AN ALTERNATIVE: 000   FOR PUDDING: 000

Beef & Red Wine Pie

SERVES 4

1 quantity quick flaky pastry (*see* p. 44), chilled
700 g/1½ lb stewing beef, cubed
4 tbsp seasoned plain flour
2 tbsp sunflower oil
2 onions, peeled and chopped

2 garlic cloves, peeled and crushed
1 tbsp freshly chopped thyme
300 ml/½ pint red wine
150 ml/¼ pint beef stock
1–2 tsp Worcestershire sauce

2 tbsp tomato ketchup
2 bay leaves
a knob of butter
225 g/8 oz button mushrooms
beaten egg or milk, to glaze
sprig of parsley, to garnish

Preheat the oven to 200°C/400°F/Gas Mark 6. Toss the beef cubes in the seasoned flour.

Heat the oil in a large heavy-based frying pan. Fry the beef in batches for about 5 minutes until golden brown. Return all of the beef to the pan and add the onions, garlic and thyme. Fry for about 10 minutes, stirring occasionally. If the beef begins to stick, add a little water.

Add the red wine and stock and bring to the boil. Stir in the Worcestershire sauce, tomato ketchup and bay leaves. Cover and simmer on a very low heat for about 1½ hours or until the beef is tender.

Heat the butter and gently sauté the mushrooms until golden brown. Add to the stew. Simmer uncovered for a further 15 minutes. Remove the bay leaves. Spoon the beef into a 1.1 litre/2 pint pie dish and reserve.

Roll out the pastry on a lightly floured surface. Cut out the lid to 5 mm/¼ inch wider than the dish. Brush the rim with the beaten egg and lay the pastry lid on top. Press to seal, then knock the edges with the back of the knife. Cut a slit in the lid and brush with the beaten egg or milk to glaze. Bake in the preheated oven for 30 minutes, or until golden brown. Garnish with the sprig of parsley and serve immediately.

Try This: FOR AN ALTERNATIVE: 68   FOR PUDDING: 322

Chilli Beef Calzone

SERVES 4

1 quantity pizza dough (*see* p. 90)
1 tbsp sunflower oil
1 onion, peeled and finely chopped
1 green pepper, deseeded and chopped
225 g/8 oz minced beef steak
420 g can chilli beans
220 g can chopped tomatoes
mixed salad leaves, to serve

Preheat the oven to 220°C/425°F/ Gas Mark 7, 15 minutes before baking. Heat the oil in a large saucepan and gently cook the onion and pepper for 5 minutes.

Add the minced beef to the saucepan and cook for 10 minutes, until browned. Add the chilli beans and tomatoes and simmer gently for 30 minutes, or until the mince is tender. Place a baking sheet into the preheated oven to heat up.

Divide the pizza dough into 4 equal pieces. Cover 3 pieces of the dough with clingfilm and roll out the other piece on a lightly floured board to a 20.5 cm/8 inch round.

Spoon a quarter of the chilli mixture on to half of the dough round and dampen the edges with a little water. Fold over the empty half of the dough and press the edges together well to seal.

Repeat this process with the remaining dough. Place on the hot baking sheet and bake for 15 minutes. Serve with the salad leaves.

Try This: FOR AN ALTERNATIVE: 56 FOR PUDDING: 312

Lamb & Pasta Pie

SERVES 8

400 g/14 oz plain white flour
pinch of salt
100 g/3½ oz margarine
100 g/3½ oz white vegetable
  fat
1 small egg, separated
50 g/2 oz butter
50 g/2 oz flour

450 ml/¾ pint milk
salt and freshly ground black
  pepper
225 g/8 oz macaroni
50 g/2 oz Cheddar cheese,
  grated
1 tbsp vegetable oil
1 onion, peeled and chopped

1 garlic clove, peeled and
  crushed
2 celery sticks, trimmed and
  chopped
450 g/1 lb lamb mince
1 tbsp tomato paste
400 g can chopped tomatoes

Preheat the oven to 190°C/375°F/Gas Mark 5, 10 minutes before cooking. Lightly oil a 20.5 cm /8 inch spring-form cake tin. Blend the flour, salt, margarine and white vegetable fat in a food processor and add cold water to make a smooth, pliable dough. Knead on a lightly floured surface, then roll out two-thirds to line the base and sides of the tin. Brush with egg white and reserve.

Melt the butter in a heavy-based pan, stir in the flour and cook for 2 minutes. Stir in the milk and cook, stirring, until a smooth, thick sauce is formed. Season to taste with salt and pepper and reserve. Bring a large pan of lightly salted water to a rolling boil. Add the macaroni and cook according to the packet instructions, or until *al dente*. Drain, then stir into the white sauce with the grated cheese. Heat the oil in a frying pan, add the onion, garlic, celery and lamb mince and cook, stirring, for 5–6 minutes. Stir in the tomato paste and tomatoes and cook for 10 minutes. Cool slightly.

Place half the pasta mixture, then all the mince in the pastry-lined tin. Top with a layer of pasta. Roll out the remaining pastry and cut out a lid. Brush the edge with water, place over the filling and pinch the edges together. Use trimmings to decorate the top of the pie. Brush the pie with beaten egg yolk and bake in the preheated oven for 50–60 minutes, covering the top with tin-foil if browning too quickly. Stand for 15 minutes before turning out. Serve immediately.

Try This: FOR AN ALTERNATIVE: 180 FOR PUDDING: 302

Chicken
Baked in a Salt Crust

SERVES 4

1.8 kg/4 lb oven-ready
  chicken
salt and freshly ground
  black pepper
1 medium onion, peeled
sprig of fresh rosemary
sprig of fresh thyme
1 bay leaf

15 g/½ oz butter, softened
1 garlic clove, peeled
  and crushed
pinch of ground paprika
finely grated rind of ½ lemon

For the salt crust:
900 g/2 lb plain flour

450 g/1 lb fine cooking salt
450 g/1 lb coarse sea salt
2 tbsp oil

To garnish:
fresh herbs
lemon slices

Preheat the oven to 170°C/325°F/Gas Mark 3. Remove the giblets if necessary and rinse the chicken with cold water. Sprinkle the inside with salt and pepper. Put the onion inside with the rosemary, thyme and bay leaf.

Mix the butter, garlic, paprika and lemon rind together. Starting at the neck end, gently ease the skin from the chicken and push the mixture under.

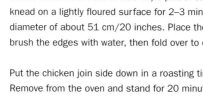

To make the salt crust, put the flour and salts in a large mixing bowl and stir together. Make a well in the centre. Pour in 600 ml/1 pint of cold water and the oil. Mix to a stiff dough, then knead on a lightly floured surface for 2–3 minutes. Roll out the pastry to a circle with a diameter of about 51 cm/20 inches. Place the chicken breast side down in the middle. Lightly brush the edges with water, then fold over to enclose. Pinch the joints together to seal.

Put the chicken join side down in a roasting tin and cook in the preheated oven for 2¾ hours. Remove from the oven and stand for 20 minutes.

Break open the hard crust and remove the chicken. Discard the crust. Remove the skin from the chicken, garnish with the fresh herbs and lemon slices. Serve the chicken immediately.

Try This: FOR AN ALTERNATIVE: 66   FOR PUDDING: 326

Chicken & Ham Pie

SERVES 6

2 quantities shortcrust
  pastry, (*see* p. 70)
1 tbsp olive oil
1 leek, trimmed and sliced
175 g/6 oz piece of bacon,
  cut into small dice
225 g/8 oz cooked boneless

chicken meat
2 avocados, peeled, pitted
  and chopped
1 tbsp lemon juice
salt and freshly ground
  black pepper
2 large eggs, beaten

150 ml/¼ pint natural yogurt
4 tbsp chicken stock
1 tbsp poppy seeds

To serve:
sliced red onion
mixed salad leaves

Preheat the oven to 200°C/400°F/Gas Mark 6. Heat the oil in a frying pan and fry the leek and bacon for 4 minutes until soft but not coloured. Transfer to a bowl and reserve.

Cut the chicken into bite-sized pieces and add to the leek and bacon. Toss the avocado in the lemon juice, add to the chicken and season to taste with salt and pepper.

Roll out half the pastry on a lightly floured surface and use to line a 18 cm/7 inch loose-bottomed deep flan tin.

Mix together 1 egg, the yogurt and the chicken stock. Mix the yogurt mixture with the chicken. Pour the chicken mixture into the pastry case.

Roll out the remaining pastry on a lightly floured surface, and cut out the lid to 5 mm/¼ inch wider than the dish. Brush the rim with the remaining beaten egg and lay the pastry lid on top, pressing to seal. Knock the edges with the back of a knife to seal further. Cut a slit in the lid and brush with the egg.

Sprinkle with the poppy seeds and bake in the preheated oven for about 30 minutes, or until the pastry is golden brown. Serve with the onion and mixed salad leaves.

Try This: FOR AN ALTERNATIVE: 68   FOR PUDDING: 324

Sauvignon Chicken & Mushroom Filo Pie

SERVES 4

1 onion, peeled and
   chopped
1 leek, trimmed and
   chopped
225 ml/8 fl oz chicken stock
3 x 175 g/6 oz chicken
   breasts
150 ml/¼ pint dry white wine
1 bay leaf

175 g/6 oz baby
   button mushrooms
2 tbsp plain flour
1 tbsp freshly
   chopped tarragon
salt and freshly ground
   black pepper
sprig of fresh parsley,
   to garnish

seasonal vegetables, to
   serve

For the topping:
75 g/3 oz (about 5 sheets)
   filo pastry
1 tbsp sunflower oil
1 tsp sesame seeds

Preheat the oven to 190°C/375°F/Gas Mark 5. Put the onion and leek in a heavy-based saucepan with 125 ml/4 fl oz of the stock. Bring to the boil, cover and simmer for 5 minutes, then uncover and cook until all the stock has evaporated and the vegetables are tender.

Cut the chicken into bite-sized cubes. Add to the pan with the remaining stock, wine and bay leaf. Cover and gently simmer for 5 minutes. Add the mushrooms and simmer for a further 5 minutes.

Blend the flour with 3 tablespoons of cold water. Stir into the pan and cook, stirring all the time until the sauce has thickened. Stir the tarragon into the sauce and season with salt and pepper.

Spoon the mixture into a 1.2 litre/2 pint pie dish, discarding the bay leaf.

Lightly brush a sheet of filo pastry with a little of the oil. Crumple the pastry slightly. Arrange on top of the filling. Repeat with the remaining filo sheets and oil, then sprinkle the top of the pie with the sesame seeds.

Bake the pie on the middle shelf of the preheated oven for 20 minutes until the filo pastry is golden and crisp. Garnish with a sprig of parsley. Serve immediately with the seasonal vegetables.

Try This: FOR AN ALTERNATIVE: 66   FOR PUDDING: 314

Smoked Haddock Tart

SERVES 6

For the shortcrust pastry:
150 g/5 oz plain flour
pinch of salt
25 g/1 oz lard or white
   vegetable fat, cut into
   small cubes
40 g/1½ oz butter or hard
   margarine, cut into cubes

For the filling:
225 g/8 oz smoked haddock,
   skinned and cubed
2 large eggs, beaten
300 ml/½ pint double cream
1 tsp Dijon mustard
freshly ground black pepper
125 g/4 oz Gruyère

cheese, grated
1 tbsp freshly snipped chives

To serve:
lemon wedges
tomato wedges
fresh green salad leaves

Preheat the oven to 190˚C/375˚F/Gas Mark 5. Sift the flour and salt into a large bowl. Add the fats and mix lightly. Using the fingertips rub into the flour until the mixture resembles breadcrumbs.

Sprinkle 1 tablespoon of cold water into the mixture and with a knife, start bringing the dough together. (It may be necessary to use the hands for the final stage.) If the dough does not form a ball instantly, add a little more water.

Put the pastry in a polythene bag and chill for at least 30 minutes.

On a lightly floured surface, roll out the pastry and use to line a 18 cm/7 inch lightly oiled quiche or flan tin. Prick the base all over with a fork and bake blind in the preheated oven for 15 minutes. Carefully remove the pastry from the oven, brush with a little of the beaten egg. Return to the oven for a further 5 minutes, then place the fish in the pastry case.

For the filling, beat together the eggs and cream. Add the mustard, black pepper and cheese and pour over the fish. Sprinkle with the chives and bake for 35–40 minutes or until the filling is golden brown and set in the centre. Serve hot or cold with the lemon, tomato wedges and salad leaves.

Try This: FOR AN ALTERNATIVE: 72   FOR PUDDING: 334

Smoked Salmon Quiche

SERVES 6

225 g/8 oz plain flour
50 g/2 oz butter
50 g/2 oz white vegetable fat
  or lard
2 tsp sunflower oil
225 g/8 oz potato, peeled
  and diced

125 g/4 oz Gruyère cheese,
  grated
75 g/3 oz smoked salmon
  trimmings
5 medium eggs, beaten
300 ml/½ pint single cream
salt and freshly ground

black pepper
1 tbsp freshly chopped flat-
  leaf parsley

To serve:
mixed salad
baby new potatoes

Preheat the oven to 200°C/400°F/Gas Mark 6. Blend the flour, butter and white vegetable fat or lard together until it resembles fine breadcrumbs. Blend again, adding sufficient water to make a firm but pliable dough. Use the dough to line a 23 cm/9 inch flan dish or tin, then chill the pastry case in the refrigerator for 30 minutes. Bake blind with baking beans for 10 minutes.

Heat the oil in a small frying pan, add the diced potato and cook for 3–4 minutes until lightly browned. Reduce the heat and cook for 2–3 minutes, or until tender. Leave to cool.

Scatter the grated cheese evenly over the base of the pastry case, then arrange the cooled potato on top. Add the smoked salmon in an even layer.

Beat the eggs with the cream and season to taste with salt and pepper. Whisk in the parsley and pour the mixture carefully into the dish.

Reduce the oven to 180°C/350°F/Gas Mark 4 and bake for about 30–40 minutes, or until the filling is set and golden. Serve hot or cold with a mixed salad and baby new potatoes.

Try This: FOR AN ALTERNATIVE: 70   FOR PUDDING: 350

Fish Puff Tart

SERVES 4

350 g/12 oz prepared puff
    pastry, thawed if frozen
150 g/5 oz smoked haddock
150 g/5 oz cod

1 tbsp pesto sauce
2 tomatoes, sliced
125 g/4 oz goats' cheese,
    sliced

1 medium egg, beaten
freshly chopped parsley, to
    garnish

Preheat the oven to 220°C/425°F/Gas Mark 7. On a lightly floured surface roll out the pastry into a 20.5 x 25.5 cm/8 x 10 inch rectangle. Draw a 18 x 23 cm/7 x 9 inch rectangle in the centre of the pastry, to form a 2.5 cm/1 inch border. (Be careful not to cut through the pastry.) Lightly cut criss-cross patterns in the border of the pastry with a knife.

Place the fish on a chopping board and with a sharp knife skin the cod and smoked haddock. Cut into thin slices.

Spread the pesto evenly over the bottom of the pastry case with the back of a spoon.

Arrange the fish, tomatoes and cheese in the pastry case and brush the pastry with the beaten egg.

Bake the tart in the preheated oven for 20–25 minutes, until the pastry is well risen, puffed and golden brown. Garnish with the chopped parsley and serve immediately.

Try This: FOR AN ALTERNATIVE: 72 FOR PUDDING: 312

Luxury Fish Pasties

SERVES 6

2 quantities of quick flaky
    pastry (*see* p. 44), chilled
125 g/4 oz butter
125 g/4oz plain flour
300 ml/½ pint milk
225 g/8 oz salmon
    fillet, skinned and cut

into chunks
1 tbsp freshly chopped
    parsley
1 tbsp freshly chopped dill
grated rind and juice of
    1 lime
225 g/8 oz peeled prawns

salt and freshly ground
    black pepper
1 small egg, beaten
1 tsp sea salt
fresh green salad leaves, to
    serve

Preheat the oven to 200°C/400°F/Gas Mark 6. Place the butter in a saucepan and slowly heat until melted. Add the flour and cook, stirring for 1 minute. Remove from the heat and gradually add the milk a little at a time, stirring between each addition. Return to the heat and simmer, stirring continuously until thickened. Remove from the heat and add the salmon, parsley, dill, lime rind, lime juice, prawns and seasoning.

Roll out the pastry on a lightly floured surface and cut out 6 x 12.5 cm/5 inch circles and 6 x 15 cm/6 inch circles.

Brush the edges of the smallest circle with the beaten egg and place two tablespoons of filling in the centre of each one. Place the larger circle over the filling and press the edges together to seal. Pinch the edge of the pastry between the forefinger and thumb to ensure a firm seal and decorative edge. Cut a slit in each parcel, brush with the beaten egg and sprinkle with sea salt.

Transfer to a baking sheet and cook in the preheated oven for 20 minutes, or until golden brown. Serve immediately with some fresh green salad leaves.

Try This: FOR AN ALTERNATIVE: 78   FOR PUDDING: 306

Russian Fish Pie

SERVES 4–6

450 g/1 lb orange roughy or
  haddock fillet
150 ml/¼ pint dry white wine
salt and freshly ground black
  pepper
75 g/3 oz butter or
  margarine
1 large onion, peeled and
  finely chopped

75 g/3 oz long-grain rice
1 tbsp freshly chopped dill
125 g/4 oz baby button
  mushrooms, quartered
125 g/4 oz peeled prawns,
  thawed if frozen
3 medium eggs, hard-boiled
  and chopped
550 g/1¼ lb ready-prepared

puff pastry, thawed if
  frozen
1 small egg, beaten with a
  pinch of salt
assorted bitter salad leaves,
  to serve

Preheat the oven to 200°C/400°F/Gas Mark 6, 15 minutes before cooking. Place the fish in a shallow frying pan with the wine, 150 ml/¼ pint water and salt and pepper. Simmer for 8–10 minutes. Strain the fish, reserving the liquid, and when cool enough to handle, flake into a bowl.

Melt the butter or margarine in a saucepan and cook the onions for 2–3 minutes, then add the rice, reserved fish liquid and dill. Season lightly. Cover and simmer for 10 minutes, then stir in the mushrooms and cook for a further 10 minutes, or until all the liquid is absorbed. Mix in the cooked fish, prawns and eggs. Leave to cool.

Roll half the pastry out on a lightly floured surface into a 23 x 30.5 cm/9 x 12 inch rectangle. Place on a dampened baking sheet and arrange the fish mixture on top, leaving a 1 cm/½ inch border. Brush the border with a little water.

Roll out the remaining pastry to a rectangle and use to cover the fish. Brush the edges lightly with a little of the beaten egg and press to seal. Roll out the pastry trimmings and use to decorate the top. Chill in the refrigerator for 30 minutes. Brush with the beaten egg and bake for 30 minutes, or until golden. Serve immediately with salad leaves.

 Try This: FOR AN ALTERNATIVE: 76   FOR PUDDING: 310

Roasted Vegetable Pie

SERVES 4

225 g/8 oz plain flour
pinch of salt
50 g/2 oz white vegetable fat
  or lard, cut into squares
50 g/2 oz butter, cut into
  squares
2 tsp herbes de Provence
1 red pepper, deseeded and
  halved

1 green pepper, deseeded
  and halved
1 yellow pepper, deseeded
  and halved
3 tbsp extra-virgin olive oil
1 aubergine, trimmed, and
  sliced
1 courgette, trimmed and
  cut into chunks

1 leek, trimmed and cut into
  chunks
1 medium egg, beaten
125 g/4 oz fresh mozzarella
  cheese, sliced
salt and freshly ground
  black pepper
sprigs of mixed herbs, to
  garnish

Preheat the oven to 220°C/425°F/Gas Mark 7. Sift the flour and salt into a large bowl, add the fats and mix lightly. Using the fingertips rub into the flour until it resembles breadcrumbs. Stir in the herbes de Provence. Sprinkle over a tablespoon of cold water and with a knife start bringing the dough together. (Perhaps using the hands for the final stage.) If the dough does not form a ball instantly, add a little more water. Place in a polythene bag and chill for 30 minutes.

Place the peppers on a baking tray and sprinkle with 1 tablespoon of oil. Roast in the preheated oven for 20 minutes or until the skins start to blacken. Brush the aubergines, courgettes and leeks with oil and place on another baking tray. Roast in the oven with the peppers for 20 minutes. Place the blackened peppers in a polythene bag and leave the skin to loosen for 5 minutes. When cool enough to handle, peel the skins off the peppers.

Roll out half the pastry on a lightly floured surface and use to line a 20.5 cm/8 inch round pie dish. Line the pastry with greaseproof paper and fill with baking beans or rice and bake blind for about 10 minutes. Remove the beans and the paper, then brush the base with a little of the beaten egg. Return to the oven for 5 minutes. Layer the cooked vegetables and the cheese in the pastry case, seasoning each layer. Roll out the remaining pastry, and cut out the lid 5 mm/¼ inch wider than the dish. Brush the rim with the beaten egg and lay the pastry on top, press to seal. Knock the edges with the back of a knife. Cut a slit in the lid and brush with the beaten egg. Bake for 30 minutes. Transfer to a large serving dish, garnish and serve immediately.

Try This: FOR AN ALTERNATIVE: 86   FOR PUDDING: 308

Stilton, Tomato & Courgette Quiche

SERVES 4

1 quantity shortcrust pastry
  (*see* p. 70)
2 large eggs, beaten
25 g/1 oz butter
1 onion, peeled and

finely chopped
1 courgette, trimmed and
  sliced
125 g/4 oz Stilton
  cheese, crumbled

6 cherry tomatoes, halved
200 ml tub crème fraîche
salt and freshly ground
  black pepper

Preheat the oven to 190°C/375°F/Gas Mark 5. On a lightly floured surface, roll out the pastry and use to line an 18 cm/7 inch lightly oiled quiche or flan tin, trimming any excess pastry with a knife.

Prick the base all over with a fork and bake blind in the preheated oven for 15 minutes. Remove the pastry from the oven and brush with a little of the beaten egg. Return to the oven for a further 5 minutes.

Heat the butter in a frying pan and gently fry the onion and courgette for about 4 minutes until soft and starting to brown. Transfer into the pastry case.

Sprinkle the Stilton over evenly and top with the halved cherry tomatoes. Beat together the eggs and crème fraîche and season to taste with salt and pepper.

Pour the filling into the pastry case and bake in the oven for 35–40 minutes, or until the filling is golden brown and set in the centre. Serve the quiche hot or cold.

Try This: FOR AN ALTERNATIVE: 84 FOR PUDDING: 324

Potato & Goats' Cheese Tart

SERVES 6

275 g/10 oz prepared
   shortcrust pastry, thawed
   if frozen
550 g/1¼ lb small waxy
   potatoes
salt and freshly ground black
   pepper

beaten egg, for brushing
2 tbsp sun-dried tomato
   paste
¼ tsp chilli powder, or to
   taste
1 large egg
150 ml/¼ pint soured cream

150 ml/¼ pint milk
2 tbsp freshly snipped
   chives
300 g/11 oz goats' cheese,
   sliced
salad and warm crusty
   bread, to serve

Preheat the oven to 190°C/375°F/Gas Mark 5, about 10 minutes before cooking. Roll the pastry out on a lightly floured surface and use to line a 23 cm/9 inch fluted flan tin. Chill in the refrigerator for 30 minutes.

Scrub the potatoes, place in a large saucepan of lightly salted water and bring to the boil. Simmer for 10–15 minutes, or until tender. Drain and reserve until cool enough to handle.

Line the pastry case with greaseproof paper and baking beans or crumpled tinfoil and bake blind in the preheated oven for 15 minutes. Remove from the oven and discard the paper and beans or tinfoil. Brush the base with a little beaten egg, then return to the oven and cook for a further 5 minutes. Remove from the oven.

Cut the potatoes into 1 cm/½ inch thick slices; reserve. Spread the sun-dried tomato paste over the base of pastry case, sprinkle with the chilli powder, then arrange the potato slices on top in a decorative pattern.

Beat together the egg, soured cream, milk and chives, then season with salt and pepper. Pour over the potatoes. Arrange the goats' cheese on top of the potatoes. Bake in the preheated oven for 30 minutes until golden brown and set. Serve immediately with salad and warm bread.

Try This: FOR AN ALTERNATIVE: 82 FOR PUDDING: 342

Leek & Potato Tart

SERVES 6

225 g/8 oz plain flour
pinch of salt
150 g/5 oz butter, cubed
50 g/2 oz walnuts, very finely
    chopped
1 large egg yolk

For the filling:
450 g/1 lb leeks, trimmed
    and thinly sliced
40 g/1½ oz butter
450 g/1 lb large new
    potatoes, scrubbed
300 ml/½ pint soured cream

3 medium eggs, lightly
    beaten
175 g/6 oz Gruyère cheese,
    grated
freshly grated nutmeg
salt and freshly ground black
    pepper
fresh chives, to garnish

Preheat the oven to 200°C/400°F/Gas Mark 6, about 15 minutes before baking. Sift the flour and salt into a bowl. Rub in the butter until the mixture resembles breadcrumbs. Stir in the nuts. Mix together the egg yolk and 3 tablespoons of cold water. Sprinkle over the dry ingredients. Mix to form a dough. Knead on a lightly floured surface for a few seconds, then wrap in clingfilm and chill in the refrigerator for 20 minutes. Roll out and use to line a 20.5 cm/8 inch spring-form tin or very deep flan tin. Chill for a further 30 minutes.

Cook the leeks in the butter over a high heat for 2–3 minutes, stirring constantly. Lower the heat, cover and cook for 25 minutes until soft, stirring occasionally. Remove the leeks from the heat.

Cook the potatoes in boiling salted water for 15 minutes, or until almost tender. Drain and thickly slice. Add to the leeks. Stir the soured cream into the leeks and potatoes, followed by the eggs, cheese, nutmeg and salt and pepper. Pour into the pastry case and bake on the middle shelf in the preheated oven for 20 minutes.

Reduce the oven temperature to 190°C/375°F/Gas Mark 5 and cook for a further 30–35 minutes, or until the filling is set. Garnish with chives and serve immediately.

Try This: FOR AN ALTERNATIVE: 84   FOR PUDDING: 326

Parsnip Tatin

SERVES 4

1 quantity shortcrust pastry
   (*see* p. 70)

For the filling:
50 g/2 oz butter
8 small parsnips, peeled

and halved
1 tbsp brown sugar
75 ml/3 fl oz apple juice

Preheat the oven to 200°C/400°F/Gas Mark 6. Heat the butter in a 20.5 cm/8 inch frying pan with metal handle.

Add the parsnips, arranging the cut side down with the narrow ends towards the centre. Sprinkle the parsnips with sugar and cook for 15 minutes, turning halfway through until golden. Add the apple juice and bring to the boil. Remove the pan from the heat.

On a lightly floured surface, roll the pastry out to a size slightly larger than the frying pan. Position the pastry over the parsnips and press down slightly to enclose the parsnips. Bake in the preheated oven for 20–25 minutes until the parsnips and pastry are golden.

Invert a warm serving plate over the pan and carefully turn the pan over to flip the tart on to the plate. Serve immediately.

Try This: FOR AN ALTERNATIVE: 276   FOR PUDDING: 340

Spinach, Pine Nut & Mascarpone Pizza

SERVES 2–4

Basic pizza dough:
225 g/8 oz strong plain flour
½ tsp salt
¼ tsp quick-acting dried
    yeast
150 ml/¼ pint warm water
1 tbsp extra-virgin olive oil

For the topping:
3 tbsp olive oil
1 large red onion, peeled
    and chopped
2 garlic cloves, peeled and
    finely sliced
450 g/1 lb frozen spinach,

thawed and drained
salt and freshly ground
    black pepper
3 tbsp passata
125 g/4 oz mascarpone
    cheese
1 tbsp toasted pine nuts

Preheat the oven to 220°C/425°F/Gas Mark 7. Sift the flour and salt into a bowl and stir in the yeast. Make a well in the centre and gradually add the water and oil to form soft dough. Knead the dough on a floured surface for about 5 minutes until smooth and elastic. Place in a lightly oiled bowl and cover with clingfilm. Leave to rise in a warm place for 1 hour.

Knock the pizza dough with your fist a few times, shape and roll out thinly on a lightly floured board. Place on a lightly floured baking sheet and lift the edge to make a little rim. Place another baking sheet into the preheated oven to heat up.

Heat half the oil in a frying pan and gently fry the onion and garlic until soft and starting to change colour.

Squeeze out any excess water from the spinach and finely chop. Add to the onion and garlic with the remaining olive oil. Season to taste with salt and pepper.

Spread the passata on the pizza dough and top with the spinach mixture. Mix the mascarpone with the pine nuts and dot over the pizza. Slide the pizza on to the hot baking sheet and bake for 15–20 minutes. Transfer to a large plate and serve immediately

Try This: FOR AN ALTERNATIVE: 92   FOR PUDDING: 344

Roquefort, Parma & Rocket Pizza

SERVES 2–4

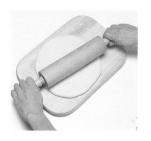

1 quantity pizza dough
(*see* p. 90)

Basic tomato sauce:
400 g can chopped tomatoes
2 garlic cloves, peeled and
crushed
grated rind of ½ lime

2 tbsp extra-virgin olive oil
2 tbsp freshly chopped basil
½ tsp sugar
salt and freshly ground
black pepper

For the topping:
125 g/4 oz Roquefort cheese,

cut into chunks
6 slices Parma ham
50 g/2 oz rocket leaves,
rinsed
1 tbsp extra-virgin olive oil
50 g/2 oz Parmesan cheese,
freshly shaved

Preheat the oven to 220°C/425°F/Gas Mark 7. Roll the pizza dough out on a lightly floured board to form a 25.5 cm/10 inch round. Lightly cover the dough and reserve while making the sauce. Place a baking sheet in the preheated oven to heat up.

Place all of the tomato sauce ingredients in a large heavy-based saucepan and slowly bring to the boil. Cover and simmer for 15 minutes, uncover and cook for a further 10 minutes until the sauce has thickened and reduced by half.

Spoon the tomato sauce over the shaped pizza dough. Place on the hot baking sheet and bake for 10 minutes.

Remove the pizza from the oven and top with the Roquefort and Parma ham, then bake for a further 10 minutes.

Toss the rocket in the olive oil and pile on to the pizza. Sprinkle with the Parmesan cheese and serve immediately.

Try This: FOR AN ALTERNATIVE: 90 FOR PUDDING: 352

Three Tomato Pizza

SERVES 2–4

1 quantity pizza dough
  (*see* p. 90)
3 plum tomatoes
8 cherry tomatoes

6 sun-dried tomatoes
pinch of sea salt
1 tbsp freshly chopped basil
2 tbsp extra-virgin olive oil

125 g/4 oz buffalo mozzarella
  cheese, sliced
freshly ground black pepper
fresh basil leaves, to garnish

Preheat the oven to 220°C/425°F/Gas Mark 7. Place a baking sheet into the oven to heat up.

Divide the prepared pizza dough into 4 equal pieces. Roll out one-quarter of the pizza dough on a lightly floured board to form a 20.5 cm/8 inch round.

Lightly cover the 3 remaining pieces of dough with clingfilm. Roll out the other 3 pieces into rounds, one at a time. While rolling out any piece of dough, keep the others covered with the clingfilm.

Slice the plum tomatoes, halve the cherry tomatoes and chop the sun-dried tomatoes into small pieces. Place a few pieces of each type of tomato on each pizza base then season to taste with the sea salt.

Sprinkle with the chopped basil and drizzle with the olive oil. Place a few slices of mozzarella on each pizza and season with black pepper.

Transfer the pizza on to the heated baking sheet and cook for 15–20 minutes, or until the cheese is golden brown and bubbling. Garnish with the basil leaves and serve immediately.

Try This: FOR AN ALTERNATIVE: 90 FOR PUDDING: 332

Fish & Shellfish

Traditional Fish Pie

SERVES 4

450 g/1 lb cod or coley fillets, skinned
450 ml/¾ pint milk
1 small onion, peeled and quartered
salt and freshly ground black pepper

900 g/2 lb potatoes, peeled and cut into chunks
100 g/3½ oz butter
125 g/4 oz large prawns
2 large eggs, hard-boiled and quartered

198 g can sweetcorn, drained
2 tbsp freshly chopped parsley
3 tbsp plain flour
50 g/2 oz Cheddar cheese, grated

Preheat the oven to 200°C/400°F/Gas Mark 6, about 15 minutes before cooking. Place the fish in a shallow frying pan, pour over 300 ml/½ pint of the milk and add the onion. Season to taste with salt and pepper. Bring to the boil and simmer for 8–10 minutes until the fish is cooked. Remove the fish with a slotted spoon and place in a 1.4 litre/2½ pint baking dish. Strain the cooking liquid and reserve.

Boil the potatoes until soft, then mash with 40 g/1½ oz of the butter and 2–3 tablespoons of the remaining milk. Reserve.

Arrange the prawns and sliced eggs on top of the fish, then scatter over the sweetcorn and sprinkle with the parsley.

Melt the remaining butter in a saucepan, stir in the flour and cook gently for 1 minute, stirring. Whisk in the reserved cooking liquid and remaining milk. Cook for 2 minutes, or until thickened, then pour over the fish mixture and cool slightly.

Spread the mashed potato over the top of the pie and sprinkle over the grated cheese. Bake in the preheated over for 30 minutes until golden. Serve immediately.

Try This: FOR AN ALTERNATIVE: 122   FOR PUDDING: 330

Fish Lasagne

SERVES 4

75 g/3 oz mushrooms
1 tsp sunflower oil
1 small onion, peeled and
  finely chopped
1 tbsp freshly
  chopped oregano
400 g can chopped tomatoes
1 tbsp tomato purée
salt and freshly ground

black pepper
450 g/1 lb cod or haddock
  fillets, skinned
9–12 sheets pre-cooked
  lasagne verde

For the topping:
1 medium egg, beaten
125 g/4 oz cottage cheese

150 ml/¼ pint low-fat
  natural yogurt
50 g/2 oz half-fat Cheddar
  cheese, grated

To serve:
mixed salad leaves
cherry tomatoes

Preheat the oven to 190°C/375°F/Gas Mark 5. Wipe the mushrooms, trim the stalks and chop. Heat the oil in a large heavy-based pan, add the onion and gently cook the onion for 3–5 minutes or until soft. Stir in the mushrooms, the oregano and the chopped tomatoes with their juice. Mix the tomato purée with 1 tablespoon of water. Stir into the pan and season to taste with salt and pepper. Bring the sauce to the boil, then simmer uncovered for 5–10 minutes.

Remove as many of the tiny pin bones as possible from the fish and cut into cubes and add to the tomato sauce mixture. Stir gently and remove the pan from the heat.

Cover the base of an ovenproof dish with 2–3 sheets of the lasagne verde. Top with half of the fish mixture. Repeat the layers finishing with the lasagne sheets.

To make the topping, mix together the beaten egg, cottage cheese and yogurt. Pour over the lasagne and sprinkle with the cheese.

Cook the lasagne in the preheated oven for 40–45 minutes or until the topping is golden brown and bubbling. Serve the lasagne immediately with the mixed salad leaves and cherry tomatoes.

Try This: FOR AN ALTERNATIVE: 102   FOR PUDDING: 370

Special Seafood Lasagne

SERVES 4–6

450 g/1 lb fresh haddock fillet, skinned
150 ml/¼ pint dry white wine
150 ml/¼ pint fish stock
½ onion, peeled and thickly sliced
1 bay leaf
75 g/3 oz butter

350 g/12 oz leeks, trimmed and thickly sliced
1 garlic clove, peeled and crushed
25 g/1 oz plain flour
150 ml/¼ pint single cream
2 tbsp freshly chopped dill
salt and freshly ground

black pepper
8–12 sheets dried lasagne verde, cooked
225 g/8 oz ready-cooked seafood cocktail
50 g/2 oz Gruyère cheese, grated

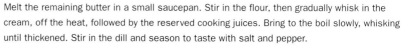

Preheat the oven to 200°C/400°F/Gas Mark 6, 15 minutes before cooking. Place the haddock in a pan with the wine, fish stock, onion and bay leaf. Bring to the boil slowly, cover and simmer gently for 5 minutes, or until the fish is opaque. Remove and flake the fish, discarding any bones. Strain the cooking juices and reserve.

Melt 50 g/2 oz of the butter in a large saucepan. Add the leeks and garlic and cook gently for 10 minutes. Remove from the pan, using a slotted draining spoon, and reserve.

Melt the remaining butter in a small saucepan. Stir in the flour, then gradually whisk in the cream, off the heat, followed by the reserved cooking juices. Bring to the boil slowly, whisking until thickened. Stir in the dill and season to taste with salt and pepper.

Spoon a little of the sauce into the base of a buttered 2.8 litre/5 pint shallow oven-proof dish. Top with a layer of lasagne, followed by the haddock, seafood cocktail and leeks. Spoon over enough sauce to cover. Continue layering up, finishing with sheets of lasagne topped with sauce.

Sprinkle over the grated Gruyère cheese and bake in the preheated oven for 40–45 minutes, or until golden-brown and bubbling. Serve immediately.

Try This: FOR AN ALTERNATIVE: 100   FOR PUDDING: 376

Foil-baked Fish

SERVES 4

For the tomato sauce:
125 ml/4 fl oz olive oil
4 garlic cloves, peeled and finely chopped
4 shallots, peeled and finely chopped
400 g can chopped Italian tomatoes

2 tbsp freshly chopped flat-leaf parsley
3 tbsp basil leaves
salt and freshly ground black pepper

700 g/1½ lb red mullet, bass or haddock fillets

450 g/1 lb live mussels
4 squids
8 large raw prawns
2 tbsp olive oil
3 tbsp dry white wine
3 tbsp freshly chopped basil leaves
lemon wedges, to garnish

Preheat oven to 180°C/350°F/Gas Mark 4, 10 minutes before cooking. Heat the olive oil and gently fry the garlic and shallots for 2 minutes. Stir in the tomatoes and simmer for 10 minutes, breaking the tomatoes down with the wooden spoon. Add the parsley and basil, season to taste with salt and pepper and cook for a further 2 minutes. Reserve and keep warm.

Lightly rinse the fish fillets and cut into 4 portions. Scrub the mussels thoroughly, removing the beard and any barnacles from the shells. Discard any mussels that are open. Clean the squid and cut into rings. Peel the prawns and remove the thin black intestinal vein that runs down the back.

Cut 4 large pieces of tinfoil, then place them on a large baking sheet and brush with olive oil. Place 1 fish portion in the centre of each piece of tinfoil. Close the tinfoil to form parcels. and bake in the preheated oven for 10 minutes, then remove.

Carefully open up the parcels and add the mussels, squid and prawns. Pour in the wine and spoon over a little of the tomato sauce. Sprinkle with the basil leaves and return to the oven and bake for 5 minutes, or until cooked thoroughly. Disgard any unopened mussels, then garnish with lemon wedges and serve with the extra tomato sauce.

Try This: FOR AN ALTERNATIVE: 102   FOR PUDDING: 372

Fried Fish with Thai Chilli Dipping Sauce

SERVES 4

1 large egg white
½ tsp curry powder or
 turmeric
3–4 tbsp cornflour
salt and freshly ground black
 pepper
4 plaice or sole fillets, about
 225 g/8 oz each

300 ml/½ pint vegetable oil

For the dipping sauce:
2 red chillies, deseeded and
 thinly sliced
2 shallots, peeled and finely
 chopped
1 tbsp freshly squeezed

 lime juice
3 tbsp Thai fish sauce
1 tbsp freshly chopped
 coriander or Thai basil

To serve:
freshly cooked rice
mixed salad leaves

To make the dipping sauce, combine all the ingredients in a bowl. Leave for at least 15 minutes.

Beat the egg white until frothy and whisk into a shallow dish.

Stir the curry powder or turmeric into the cornflour in a bowl and season to taste with salt and pepper. Dip each fish fillet in the beaten egg white, dust lightly on both sides with the cornflour mixture and place on a wire rack.

Heat a wok or large frying pan, add the oil and heat to 180˚C/350˚F. Add 1 or 2 fillets and fry for 5 minutes, or until crisp and golden, turning once during cooking.

Using a slotted spatula, carefully remove the cooked fish and drain on absorbent kitchen paper. Keep warm while frying the remaining fillets.

Arrange the fillets on warmed individual plates and serve immediately with the dipping sauce, rice and salad.

Try This: FOR AN ALTERNATIVE: 136 FOR PUDDING: 360

Mediterranean Fish Stew

SERVES 4–6

4 tbsp olive oil
1 onion, peeled and finely sliced
5 garlic cloves, peeled and finely sliced
1 fennel bulb, trimmed and finely chopped
3 celery sticks, trimmed and finely chopped

400 g can chopped tomatoes with Italian herbs
1 tbsp freshly chopped oregano
1 bay leaf
zest and juice of 1 orange
1 tsp saffron strands
750 ml/1¼ pints fish stock
3 tbsp dry vermouth

salt and freshly ground black pepper
225 g/8 oz thick haddock fillets
225 g/8 oz sea bass or bream fillets
225 g/8 oz raw tiger prawns, peeled
crusty bread, to serve

Heat the olive oil in a large saucepan. Add the onion, garlic, fennel and celery and cook over a low heat for 15 minutes, stirring frequently until the vegetables are soft and just beginning to turn brown.

Add the canned tomatoes with their juice, oregano, bay leaf, orange zest and juice with the saffron strands. Bring to the boil, then reduce the heat and simmer for 5 minutes. Add the fish stock, vermouth and season to taste with salt and pepper. Bring to the boil. Reduce the heat and simmer for 20 minutes.

Wipe or rinse the haddock and bass fillets and remove as many of the bones as possible. Place on a chopping board and cut into 5 cm/2 inch cubes. Add to the saucepan and cook for 3 minutes. Add the prawns and cook for a further 5 minutes. Adjust the seasoning to taste and serve with crusty bread.

Try This: FOR AN ALTERNATIVE: 138   FOR PUDDING: 356

Fish Balls in
Hot Yellow Bean Sauce

SERVES 4

450 g/1 lb skinless white fish
    fillets, such as cod or
    haddock, cut into pieces
½ tsp salt
1 tbsp cornflour
2 spring onions, trimmed
    and chopped
1 tbsp freshly chopped
    coriander

1 tsp soy sauce
1 medium egg white
freshly ground black pepper
sprig of tarragon, to garnish
freshly cooked rice, to serve

For the yellow bean sauce:
75 ml/3 fl oz fish or chicken
    stock

1–2 tsp yellow bean sauce
2 tbsp soy sauce
1–2 tbsp Chinese rice wine
    or dry sherry
1 tsp chilli bean sauce, or to
    taste
1 tsp sesame oil
1 tsp sugar (optional)

Put the fish pieces, salt, cornflour, spring onions, coriander, soy sauce and egg white into a food processor, season to taste with pepper, then blend until a smooth paste forms, scraping down the sides of the bowl occasionally.

With dampened hands, shape the mixture into 2.5 cm/1 inch balls. Transfer to a baking tray and chill in the refrigerator for at least 30 minutes.

Bring a large saucepan of water to simmering point. Working in 2 or 3 batches, drop in the fish balls and poach gently for 3–4 minutes or until they float to the top. Transfer to absorbent kitchen paper to drain.

Put all the sauce ingredients in a wok or large frying pan and bring to the boil. Add the fish balls to the sauce and stir-fry gently for 2–3 minutes until piping hot. Transfer to a warmed serving dish, garnish with sprigs of tarragon and serve immediately with freshly cooked rice.

Try This: FOR AN ALTERNATIVE: 106   FOR PUDDING: 318

Battered Cod & Chunky Chips

SERVES 4

15 g/½ oz fresh yeast
300 ml/½ pint beer
225 g/8 oz plain flour
1 tsp salt
700 g/1½ lb potatoes
450 ml/¾ pint groundnut oil

4 cod fillets, about 225 g/8 oz
    each, skinned and boned
2 tbsp seasoned plain flour

To garnish:
lemon wedges

sprigs of flat-leaf parsley

To serve:
tomato ketchup
vinegar

Dissolve the yeast with a little of the beer in a jug and mix to a paste. Pour in the remaining beer, whisking all the time until smooth. Place the flour and salt in a bowl, and gradually pour in the beer mixture, whisking continuously to make a thick smooth batter. Cover the bowl and allow the batter to stand at room temperature for 1 hour.

Peel the potatoes and cut into thick slices. Cut each slice lengthways to make chunky chips. Place them in a non-stick frying pan and heat, shaking the pan until all the moisture has evaporated. Turn them onto absorbent kitchen paper to dry off.

Heat the oil to 180˚C/350˚F, then fry the chips a few at a time for 4–5 minutes until crisp and golden. Drain on absorbent kitchen paper and keep warm.

Pat the cod fillets dry, then coat in the flour. Dip the floured fillets into the reserved batter. Fry for 2–3 minutes until cooked and crisp, then drain. Garnish with lemon wedges and parsley and serve immediately with the chips, tomato ketchup and vinegar.

Try This: FOR AN ALTERNATIVE: 136   FOR PUDDING: 300

Seared Pancetta-wrapped Cod

SERVES 4

4 x 175 g/6 oz thick cod fillets
4 very thin slices of pancetta
3 tbsp capers in vinegar
1 tbsp of vegetable or
   sunflower oil

2 tbsp lemon juice
1 tbsp olive oil
freshly ground black pepper
1 tbsp freshly chopped
   parsley, to garnish

To serve:
freshly cooked vegetables
new potatoes

Wipe the cod fillets and wrap each one with the pancetta. Secure each fillet with a cocktail stick and reserve.

Drain the capers and soak in cold water for 10 minutes to remove any excess salt, then drain and reserve.

Heat the oil in a large frying pan and sear the wrapped pieces of cod fillet for about 3 minutes on each side, turning carefully with a fish slice so as not to break up the fish. Lower the heat then continue to cook for 2–3 minutes or until the fish is cooked thoroughly.

Meanwhile, place the reserved capers, lemon juice and olive oil into a small saucepan. Grind over the black pepper.

Place the saucepan over a low heat and bring to a gentle simmer, stirring continuously for 2–3 minutes.

Once the fish is cooked, leave to rest for a couple of minutes, then garnish with the parsley and serve with the warm caper dressing, freshly cooked vegetables and new potatoes.

Try This: FOR AN ALTERNATIVE: 116   FOR PUDDING: 370

Roasted Cod with Saffron Aïoli

SERVES 4

For the saffron aïoli:
2 garlic cloves, peeled
¼ tsp saffron strands
sea salt, to taste
1 medium egg yolk
200 ml/7 fl oz extra-virgin
olive oil
2 tbsp lemon juice

For the marinade:
2 tbsp olive oil
4 garlic cloves, peeled and
finely chopped
1 red onion, peeled and
finely chopped
1 tbsp freshly chopped
rosemary

2 tbsp freshly chopped thyme

4–6 sprigs of fresh rosemary
1 lemon, sliced
4 x 175 g/6 oz thick cod
fillets with skin
freshly cooked vegtables,
to serve

Preheat oven to 180°C/350°F/Gas Mark 4, 10 minutes before cooking. Crush the garlic, saffron and a pinch of salt in a pestle and mortar to form a paste. Place in a blender with the egg yolk and blend for 30 seconds. With the motor running, slowly add the olive oil in a thin, steady stream until the mayonnaise is smooth and thick. Spoon into a small bowl and stir in the lemon juice. Cover and leave in the refrigerator until required.

Combine the olive oil, garlic, red onion, rosemary and thyme for the marinade and leave to infuse for about 10 minutes.

Place the sprigs of rosemary and slices of lemon in the bottom of a lightly oiled roasting tin. Add the cod, skinned-side up. Pour over the prepared marinade and leave to marinate in the refrigerator for 15–20 minutes. Bake in the preheated oven for 15–20 minutes, or until the cod is cooked and the flesh flakes easily with a fork. Leave the cod to rest for 1 minute before serving with the saffron aïoli and vegetables.

Try This: FOR AN ALTERNATIVE: 114   FOR PUDDING: 364

Saucy Cod & Pasta Bake

SERVES 4

450 g/1 lb cod fillets, skinned
2 tbsp sunflower oil
1 onion, peeled and
chopped
4 rashers smoked streaky
bacon, rind removed and
chopped
150 g/5 oz baby button
mushrooms, wiped

2 celery sticks, trimmed and
thinly sliced
2 small courgettes, halved
lengthwise and sliced
400 g can chopped tomatoes
100 ml/3½ fl oz fish stock or
dry white wine
1 tbsp freshly chopped
tarragon

salt and freshly ground black
pepper

For the pasta topping:
225–275 g/8–10 oz pasta
shells
25 g/1 oz butter
4 tbsp plain flour
450 ml/¾ pint milk

Preheat the oven to 200°C/400°F/Gas Mark 6, 15 minutes before cooking. Cut the cod into bite-sized pieces and reserve.

Heat the sunflower oil in a large saucepan, add the onion and bacon and cook for 7–8 minutes. Add the mushrooms and celery and cook for 5 minutes, or until fairly soft. Add the courgettes and tomatoes to the bacon mixture and pour in the fish stock or wine. Bring to the boil, then simmer uncovered for 5 minutes, or until the sauce has thickened slightly. Remove from the heat and stir in the cod pieces and the tarragon. Season to taste with salt and pepper, then spoon into a large oiled baking dish.

Meanwhile, bring a large pan of lightly salted water to a rolling boil. Add the pasta shells and cook, according to the packet instructions, or until *al dente.*

For the topping, place the butter and flour in a saucepan and pour in the milk. Bring to the boil slowly, whisking until thickened and smooth. Drain the pasta thoroughly, and stir into the sauce. Spoon carefully over the fish and vegetables. Place in the preheated oven and bake for 20–25 minutes, or until the top is lightly browned and bubbling.

Try This: FOR AN ALTERNATIVE: 128   FOR PUDDING: 318

Crispy Cod Cannelloni

SERVES 4

1 tbsp olive oil
8 dried cannelloni tubes
25 g/1 oz unsalted butter
225 g/8 oz button
  mushrooms, thinly sliced
175 g/6 oz leeks, trimmed
  and finely chopped

175 g/6 oz cod, skinned and
  diced
175 g/6 oz cream cheese
salt and freshly ground black
  pepper
15 g/½ oz Parmesan cheese,
  grated

50 g/2 oz fine fresh white
  breadcrumbs
3 tbsp plain flour
1 medium egg, lightly beaten
oil for deep frying
fresh herbs or salad leaves,
  to serve

Add 1 teaspoon of the olive oil to a large pan of lightly salted water and bring to a rolling boil. Add the cannelloni tubes and cook, uncovered, for 5 minutes. Drain and leave in a bowl of cold water.

Melt the butter with the remaining oil in a saucepan. Add the mushrooms and leeks and cook gently for 5 minutes. Turn up the heat and cook for 1–2 minutes, or until the mixture is fairly dry. Add the cod and cook, stirring, for 2–3 minutes, or until the fish is opaque. Add the cream cheese to the pan and stir until melted. Season to taste with salt and pepper, then leave the cod mixture to cool.

Drain the cannelloni. Using a piping bag without a nozzle or a spoon, fill the cannelloni with the cod mixture.

Mix the Parmesan cheese and breadcrumbs together on a plate. Dip the filled cannelloni into the flour, then into the beaten egg and finally into the breadcrumb mixture. Dip the ends twice to ensure they are thoroughly coated. Chill in the refrigerator for 30 minutes.

Heat the oil for deep frying to 180°C/350°F. Fry the stuffed cannelloni in batches for 2–3 minutes, or until the coating is crisp and golden-brown. Drain on absorbent kitchen paper and serve immediately with fresh herbs or salad leaves.

Try This: FOR AN ALTERNATIVE: 124   FOR PUDDING: 354

Smoked Haddock Kedgeree

SERVES 4

450 g/1 lb smoked haddock
    fillets
50 g/2 oz butter
1 onion, peeled and finely
    chopped
2 tsp mild curry powder

175 g/6 oz long-grain rice
450 ml/¾ pint fish or
    vegetable stock, heated
2 large eggs, hard-boiled
    and shelled
2 tbsp freshly chopped parsley

2 tbsp whipping cream
    (optional)
salt and freshly ground black
    pepper
pinch of cayenne pepper

Place the haddock in a shallow frying pan and cover with 300 ml/½ pint water. Simmer gently for 8–10 minutes, or until the fish is cooked. Drain, then remove all the skin and bones from the fish and flake into a dish. Keep warm.

Melt the butter in a saucepan and add the chopped onion and curry powder. Cook, stirring, for 3–4 minutes, or until the onion is soft, then stir in the rice. Cook for a further minute, stirring continuously, then stir in the hot stock.

Cover and simmer gently for 15 minutes, or until the rice has absorbed all the liquid. Cut the eggs into quarters or eighths and add half to the mixture with half the parsley.

Carefully fold in the cooked fish to the mixture and add the cream, if using. Season to taste with salt and pepper. Heat the kedgeree through briefly until piping hot.

Transfer the mixture to a large dish and garnish with the remaining quartered eggs, parsley and serve with a pinch of cayenne pepper. Serve immediately.

Try This: FOR AN ALTERNATIVE: 98   FOR PUDDING: 296

Haddock with an Olive Crust

SERVES 4

12 pitted black olives,
   finely chopped
75 g/3 oz fresh white
   breadcrumbs
1 tbsp freshly
   chopped tarragon

1 garlic clove, peeled
   and crushed
3 spring onions, trimmed
   and finely chopped
1 tbsp olive oil
4 x 175 g/6 oz thick skinless

haddock fillets

To serve:
freshly cooked carrots
freshly cooked beans

Preheat the oven to 190°C/375°F/Gas Mark 5. Place the black olives in a small bowl with the breadcrumbs and add the chopped tarragon.

Add the garlic to the olives with the chopped spring onions and the olive oil. Mix together lightly.

Wipe the fillets with either a clean damp cloth or damp kitchen paper, then place on a lightly oiled baking sheet.

Place spoonfuls of the olive and breadcrumb mixture on top of each fillet and press the mixture down lightly and evenly over the top of the fish.

Bake the fish in the preheated oven for 20–25 minutes or until the fish is cooked thoroughly and the topping is golden brown. Serve immediately with the freshly cooked carrots and beans.

Try This: FOR AN ALTERNATIVE: 126   FOR PUDDING: 344

Smoked Haddock Rosti

SERVES 4

450 g/1 lb potatoes, peeled and coarsely grated
1 large onion, peeled and coarsely grated
2–3 garlic cloves, peeled and crushed

450 g/1 lb smoked haddock
1 tbsp olive oil
salt and freshly ground black pepper
finely grated rind of ½ lemon
1 tbsp freshly chopped parsley

2 tbsp half-fat crème fraîche

To serve:
mixed salad leaves
lemon wedges

Dry the grated potatoes in a clean tea towel. Rinse the grated onion thoroughly in cold water, dry in a clean tea towel and add to the potatoes. Stir the garlic into the potato mixture.

Skin the smoked haddock and remove as many of the tiny pin bones as possible. Cut into thin slices and reserve.

Heat the oil in a non-stick frying pan. Add half the potatoes and press well down in the frying pan. Season to taste with salt and pepper.

Add a layer of fish and a sprinkling of lemon rind, parsley and a little black pepper.

Top with the remaining potatoes and press down firmly. Cover with a sheet of tinfoil and cook on the lowest heat for 25–30 minutes.

Preheat the grill 2–3 minutes before the end of cooking time. Remove the tinfoil and place the rosti under the grill to brown. Turn out on to a warmed serving dish, and serve immediately with spoonfuls of crème fraîche, lemon wedges and mixed salad leaves.

Try This: FOR AN ALTERNATIVE: 132 FOR PUDDING: 368

Pappardelle with Smoked Haddock & Blue Cheese Sauce

SERVES 4

350 g/12 oz smoked haddock
2 bay leaves
300 ml/½ pint milk
400 g/14 oz pappardelle or
   tagliatelle
25 g/1 oz butter
25 g/1 oz plain flour

150 ml/¼ pint single cream
   or extra milk
125 g/4 oz Dolcelatte cheese
   or Gorgonzola, cut into
   small pieces
¼ tsp freshly grated nutmeg
salt and freshly ground

black pepper
40 g/1½ oz toasted walnuts,
   chopped
1 tbsp freshly chopped
   parsley

Place the smoked haddock in a saucepan with 1 bay leaf and pour in the milk. Bring to the boil slowly, cover and simmer for 6–7 minutes, or until the fish is opaque. Remove and roughly flake the fish, discarding the skin and any bones. Strain the milk and reserve.

Bring a large pan of lightly salted water to a rolling boil. Add the pasta and cook according to the packet instructions, or until *al dente*.

Meanwhile, melt the butter in a pan, stir in the flour, then slowly whisk in the single cream or milk if preferred. Stir in the reserved warm milk and add the remaining bay leaf. Bring to the boil, whisking all the time until smooth and thick. Gently simmer for 3–4 minutes, stirring frequently. Discard the bay leaf.

Add the Dolcelatte or Gorgonzola cheese to the sauce. Heat gently, stirring until melted. Add the flaked haddock and season to taste with nutmeg and salt and pepper.

Drain the pasta thoroughly and return to the pan. Add the sauce and toss gently to coat, taking care not to break up the flakes of fish. Tip into a warmed serving bowl, sprinkle with toasted walnuts and parsley and serve immediately

 Try This: FOR AN ALTERNATIVE: 118   FOR PUDDING: 352

Ratatouille Mackerel

SERVES 4

1 red pepper
1 tbsp olive oil
1 red onion, peeled
1 garlic clove, peeled and
   thinly sliced
2 courgettes, trimmed and

cut into thick slices
400 g can chopped tomatoes
sea salt and freshly ground
   black pepper
4 x 275 g/10 oz small
   mackerel, cleaned and

heads removed
spray of olive oil
lemon juice for drizzling
12 fresh basil leaves
couscous or rice mixed with
   chopped parsley, to serve

Preheat the oven to 190°C/375°F/Gas Mark 5. Cut the top off the red pepper, remove the seeds and membrane, then cut into chunks. Cut the red onion into thick wedges.

Heat the oil in a large pan and cook the onion and garlic for 5 minutes or until beginning to soften. Add the pepper chunks and courgettes slices and cook for a further 5 minutes.

Pour in the chopped tomatoes with their juice and cook for a further 5 minutes. Season to taste with salt and pepper and pour into an ovenproof dish.

Season the fish with salt and pepper and arrange on top of the vegetables. Spray with a little olive oil and lemon juice. Cover and cook in the preheated oven for 20 minutes.

Remove the cover, add the basil leaves and return to the oven for a further 5 minutes. Serve immediately with couscous or rice mixed with parsley.

 Try This: FOR AN ALTERNATIVE: 138   FOR PUDDING: 366

Smoked Mackerel & Pasta Frittata

SERVES 4

25 g/1 oz tricolore pasta
  spirals or shells
225 g/8 oz smoked mackerel
6 medium eggs
3 tbsp milk
2 tsp wholegrain mustard
2 tbsp freshly chopped parsley

salt and freshly ground
  black pepper
25 g/1 oz unsalted butter
6 spring onions, trimmed
  and diagonally sliced
50 g/2 oz frozen peas,
  thawed

75 g/3 oz mature Cheddar
  cheese, grated

To serve:
green salad
warm crusty bread

Preheat the grill to high just before cooking. Bring a pan of lightly salted water to a rolling boil. Add the pasta and cook according to the packet instructions, or until *al dente*. Drain thoroughly and reserve.

Remove the skin from the mackerel and break the fish into large flakes, discarding any bones, and reserve.

Place the eggs, milk, mustard and parsley in a bowl and whisk together. Season with just a little salt and plenty of freshly ground black pepper and reserve.

Melt the butter in a large, heavy-based frying pan. Cook the spring onions gently for 3–4 minutes, until soft. Pour in the egg mixture, then add the drained pasta, peas and half of the mackerel.

Gently stir the mixture in the pan for 1–2 minutes, or until beginning to set. Stop stirring and cook for about 1 minute until the underneath is golden-brown.

Scatter the remaining mackerel over the frittata, followed by the grated cheese. Place under the preheated grill for about 1½ minutes, or until golden-brown and set. Cut into wedges and serve immediately with salad and crusty bread.

Try This: FOR AN ALTERNATIVE: 126   FOR PUDDING: 364

Citrus–grilled Plaice

SERVES 4

1 tsp sunflower oil
1 onion, peeled and
    chopped
1 orange pepper, deseeded
    and chopped
175 g/6 oz long-grain rice
150 ml/¼ pint orange juice

2 tbsp lemon juice
225 ml/8 fl oz vegetable
    stock
spray of oil
4 x 175 g/6 oz plaice
    fillets, skinned
1 orange

1 lemon
25 g/1 oz butter or spread
2 tbsp freshly
    chopped tarragon
salt and freshly ground
    black pepper
lemon wedges, to garnish

Heat the oil in a large frying pan, then sauté the onion, pepper and rice for 2 minutes.

Add the orange and lemon juice and bring to the boil. Reduce the heat, add half the stock and simmer for 15–20 minutes, or until the rice is tender, adding the remaining stock as necessary.

Preheat the grill. Finely spray the base of the grill pan with oil. Place the plaice fillets in the base and reserve.

Finely grate the orange and lemon rind. Squeeze the juice from half of each fruit.

Melt the butter or spread in a small saucepan. Add the grated rind, juice and half of the tarragon and use to baste the plaice fillets.

Cook one side only of the fish under the preheated grill at a medium heat for 4–6 minutes, basting continuously.

Once the rice is cooked, stir in the remaining tarragon and season to taste with salt and pepper. Garnish the fish with the lemon wedges and serve immediately with the rice.

Try This: FOR AN ALTERNATIVE: 130   FOR PUDDING: 330

Goujons of Plaice with Tartare Sauce

SERVES 4

75 g/3 oz fresh white breadcrumbs
3 tbsp freshly grated Parmesan cheese
salt and freshly ground black pepper
1 tbsp dried oregano
1 medium egg
450 g/1 lb plaice fillets

300 ml/½ pint vegetable oil for deep frying
fat chips, to serve

For the tartare sauce:
200 ml/7 fl oz prepared mayonnaise
50 g/2 oz gherkins, finely chopped

2 tbsp freshly snipped chives
1 garlic clove, peeled and crushed
2–3 tbsp capers, drained and chopped
pinch of cayenne pepper

Mix together the breadcrumbs, Parmesan cheese, seasoning and oregano on a large plate. Lightly beat the egg in a shallow dish. Then, using a sharp knife, cut the plaice fillets into thick strips. Coat the plaice strips in the beaten egg, allowing any excess to drip back into the dish, then dip the strips into the breadcrumbs until well coated. Place the goujons on a baking sheet, cover and chill in the refrigerator for 30 minutes.

Meanwhile, to make the tartare sauce, mix together the mayonnaise, gherkins, chives, garlic, capers and cayenne pepper. Stir, then season to taste with salt and pepper. Place in a bowl, cover loosely and store in the refrigerator until required.

Pour the oil into a large wok. Heat to 190˚C/375˚F, or until a small cube of bread turns golden and crisp in about 30 seconds. Cook the plaice goujons in batches for about 4 minutes, turning occasionally, until golden. Using a slotted spoon, remove and drain on absorbent kitchen paper. Serve immediately with the tartare sauce and chips.

Try This: FOR AN ALTERNATIVE: 112   FOR PUDDING: 346

Chunky Halibut Casserole

SERVES 6

50 g/2 oz butter or margarine
2 large onions, peeled and sliced into rings
1 red pepper, deseeded and roughly chopped
450 g/1 lb potatoes, peeled
450 g/1 lb courgettes,

trimmed and thickly sliced
2 tbsp plain flour
1 tbsp paprika
2 tsp vegetable oil
300 ml/½ pint white wine
150 ml/¼ pint fish stock
400 g can chopped tomatoes
2 tbsp freshly chopped basil

salt and freshly ground black pepper
450 g/1 lb halibut fillet, skinned and cut into 2.5 cm/ 1 inch cubes
sprigs of fresh basil, to garnish
freshly cooked rice, to serve

Melt the butter or margarine in a large saucepan, add the onions and pepper and cook for 5 minutes, or until softened.

Cut the peeled potatoes into 2.5 cm/1 inch dice, rinse lightly and shake dry, then add them to the onions and pepper in the saucepan. Add the courgettes and cook, stirring frequently, for a further 2–3 minutes.

Sprinkle the flour, paprika and vegetable oil into the saucepan and cook, stirring continuously, for 1 minute. Pour in 150 ml/¼ pint of the wine, with the stock and the chopped tomatoes, and bring to the boil.

Add the basil to the casserole, season to taste with salt and pepper and cover. Simmer for 15 minutes, then add the halibut and the remaining wine and simmer very gently for a further 5–7 minutes, or until the fish and vegetables are just tender. Garnish with basil sprigs and serve immediately with freshly cooked rice.

Try This: FOR AN ALTERNATIVE: 108   FOR PUDDING: 298

Salmon Fish Cakes

SERVES 4

450 g/1 lb salmon fillet, skinned
salt and freshly ground black pepper
450 g/1 lb potatoes, peeled and cut into chunks
25 g/1 oz butter
1 tbsp milk

2 medium tomatoes, skinned, deseeded and chopped
2 tbsp freshly chopped parsley
75 g/3 oz wholemeal breadcrumbs
25 g/1 oz Cheddar cheese, grated

2 tbsp plain flour
2 medium eggs, beaten
3–4 tbsp vegetable oil

To serve:
ready-made raita
sprigs of fresh mint

Place the salmon in a shallow frying pan and cover with water. Season to taste with salt and pepper and simmer for 8–10 minutes until the fish is cooked. Drain and flake into a bowl.

Boil the potatoes in lightly salted water until soft, then drain. Mash with the butter and milk until smooth. Add the potato to the bowl of fish and stir in the tomatoes and half the parsley. Adjust the seasoning to taste. Chill the mixture in the refrigerator for at least 2 hours to firm up.

Mix the breadcrumbs with the grated cheese and the remaining parsley. When the fish mixture is firm, form into 8 flat cakes. First, lightly coat the fish cakes in the flour, then dip into the beaten egg, allowing any excess to drip back into the bowl. Finally, press into the breadcrumb mixture until well coated.

Heat a little of the oil in a frying pan and fry the fish cakes in batches for 2–3 minutes on each side until golden and crisp, adding more oil if necessary. Serve with raita garnished with sprigs of mint.

Try This: FOR AN ALTERNATIVE: 146   FOR PUDDING: 302

Pan–fried Salmon with Herb Risotto

SERVES 4

4 x 175 g/6 oz salmon fillets
3–4 tbsp plain flour
1 tsp dried mustard powder
salt and freshly ground black
   pepper
2 tbsp olive oil
3 shallots, peeled and
   chopped

225 g/8 oz Arborio rice
150 ml/¼ pint dry white wine
1.4 litres/2½ pints vegetable
   or fish stock
50 g/2 oz butter
2 tbsp freshly snipped chives
2 tbsp freshly chopped dill
2 tbsp freshly chopped flat-

   leaf parsley
knob of butter

To garnish:
slices of lemon
sprigs of fresh dill
tomato salad, to serve

Wipe the salmon fillets with a clean, damp cloth. Mix together the flour, mustard powder and seasoning on a large plate and use to coat the salmon fillets and reserve.

Heat half the olive oil in a large frying pan and fry the shallots for 5 minutes until softened, but not coloured. Add the rice and stir for 1 minute, then slowly add the wine, bring to the boil and boil rapidly until reduced by half.

Bring the stock to a gentle simmer, then add to the rice, a ladleful at a time. Cook, stirring frequently, until all the stock has been added and the rice is cooked but still retains a bite. Stir in the butter and freshly chopped herbs and season to taste with salt and pepper.

Heat the remaining olive oil and the knob of butter in a large griddle pan, add the salmon fillets and cook for 2–3 minutes on each side, or until cooked. Arrange the herb risotto on warm serving plates and top with the salmon. Garnish with slices of lemon and sprigs of dill and serve immediately with a tomato salad.

Try This: FOR AN ALTERNATIVE: 144   FOR PUDDING: 364

Stir-fried Salmon with Peas

SERVES 4

450 g/1 lb salmon fillet
salt
6 slices streaky bacon
1 tbsp vegetable oil
50 ml/2 fl oz chicken or fish
    stock
2 tbsp dark soy sauce

2 tbsp Chinese rice wine or
    dry sherry
1 tsp sugar
75 g/3 oz frozen peas,
    thawed
1–2 tbsp freshly shredded
    mint

1 tsp cornflour
sprigs of fresh mint, to
    garnish
freshly cooked noodles,
    to serve

Wipe and skin the salmon fillet and remove any pin bones. Slice into 2.5 cm/1 inch strips, place on a plate and sprinkle with salt. Leave for 20 minutes, then pat dry with absorbent kitchen paper and reserve.

Remove any cartilage from the bacon, cut into small dice and reserve.

Heat a wok or large frying pan over a high heat, then add the oil and when hot, add the bacon and stir-fry for 3 minutes or until crisp and golden. Push to one side and add the strips of salmon. Stir-fry gently for 2 minutes or until the flesh is opaque.

Pour the chicken or fish stock, soy sauce and Chinese rice wine or sherry into the wok, then stir in the sugar, peas and freshly shredded mint.

Blend the cornflour with 1 tablespoon of water to form a smooth paste and stir into the sauce. Bring to the boil, reduce the heat and simmer for 1 minute, or until slightly thickened and smooth. Garnish and serve immediately with noodles.

Try This: FOR AN ALTERNATIVE: 142   FOR PUDDING: 306

Tuna Fish Burgers

MAKES 8

450 g/1 lb potatoes, peeled and cut into chunks
50 g/2 oz butter
2 tbsp milk
400 g can tuna in oil
1 spring onion, trimmed and finely chopped

1 tbsp freshly chopped parsley
salt and freshly ground black pepper
2 medium eggs, beaten
2 tbsp seasoned plain flour
125 g/4 oz fresh white breadcrumbs

4 tbsp vegetable oil
4 sesame seed baps (optional)

To serve:
fat chips
mixed salad
tomato chutney

Place the potatoes in a large saucepan, cover with boiling water and simmer until soft. Drain, then mash with 40 g/1½ oz of the butter and the milk. Turn into a large bowl. Drain the tuna, discarding the oil and flake into the bowl of potato. Stir well to mix.

Add the spring onions and parsley to the mixture and season to taste with salt and pepper. Add 1 tablespoon of the beaten egg to bind the mixture together. Chill in the refrigerator for at least 1 hour.

Shape the chilled mixture with your hands into 4 large burgers. First, coat the burgers with seasoned flour, then brush them with the remaining beaten egg, allowing any excess to drip back into the bowl. Finally, coat them evenly in the breadcrumbs, pressing the crumbs on with your hands, if necessary.

Heat a little of the oil in a frying pan and fry the burgers for 2–3 minutes on each side until golden, adding more oil if necessary. Drain on absorbent kitchen paper and serve hot in baps, if using, with chips, mixed salad and chutney.

Try This: FOR AN ALTERNATIVE: 140 FOR PUDDING: 328

Tuna Cannelloni

SERVES 4

1 tbsp olive oil
6 spring onions, trimmed
and finely sliced
1 sweet Mediterranean red
pepper, deseeded and
finely chopped
200 g can tuna in brine

250 g tub ricotta cheese
zest and juice of 1 lemon
1 tbsp freshly snipped chives
salt and freshly ground black
pepper
8 dried cannelloni tubes
1 medium egg, beaten

125 g/4 oz cottage cheese
150 ml/¼ pint natural yogurt
pinch of freshly grated
nutmeg
50 g/2 oz mozzarella cheese,
grated
tossed green salad, to serve

Preheat oven to 180°C/375°F/Gas Mark 5, 10 minutes before cooking. Heat the olive oil in a frying pan and cook the spring onions and pepper until soft. Remove from the pan with a slotted draining spoon and place in large bowl.

Drain the tuna, then stir into the spring onions and pepper. Beat the ricotta cheese with the lemon zest and juice, and the snipped chives, and season to taste with salt and pepper until soft and blended. Add to the tuna and mix together. If the mixture is still a little stiff, add a little extra lemon juice.

With a teaspoon, carefully spoon the mixture into the cannelloni tubes, then lay the filled tubes in a lightly oiled shallow ovenproof dish. Beat the egg, cottage cheese, natural yogurt and nutmeg together and pour over the cannelloni. Sprinkle with the grated mozzarella cheese and bake in the preheated oven for 15–20 minutes, or until the topping is golden brown and bubbling. Serve immediately with a tossed green salad.

Try This: FOR AN ALTERNATIVE: 132 FOR PUDDING: 370

Potato Boulangere with Sea Bass

SERVES 2

450 g/1 lb potatoes, peeled and thinly sliced
1 large onion, peeled and thinly sliced

salt and freshly ground black pepper
300 ml/½ pint fish or vegetable stock

75 g/3 oz butter or margarine
350 g/12 oz sea bass fillets
sprigs of fresh flat-leaf parsley, to garnish

Preheat the oven to 200°C/400°F/Gas Mark 6. Lightly grease a shallow 1.4 litre/2½ pint baking dish with oil or butter. Layer the potato slices and onions alternately in the prepared dish, seasoning each layer with salt and pepper.

Pour the stock over the top, then cut 50 g/2 oz of the butter or margarine into small pieces and dot over the top layer. Bake in the preheated oven for 50–60 minutes. Do not cover the dish at this stage.

Lightly rinse the sea bass fillets and pat dry on absorbent kitchen paper. Cook in a griddle, or heat the remaining butter or margarine in a frying pan and shallow fry the fish fillets for 3–4 minutes per side, flesh side first. Remove from the pan with a slotted spatula and drain on absorbent kitchen paper.

Remove the partly cooked potato and onion mixture from the oven and place the fish on the top. Cover with tinfoil and return to the oven for 10 minutes until heated through. Garnish with sprigs of parsley and serve immediately.

Try This: FOR AN ALTERNATIVE: 156 FOR PUDDING: 304

Roasted Monkfish with Parma Ham

SERVES 4

700 g/1½ lb monkfish tail
sea salt and freshly ground
   black pepper
4 bay leaves
4 slices fontina cheese, rind
   removed

8 slices Parma ham
225 g/8 oz angel hair pasta
50 g/2 oz butter
the zest and juice of 1 lemon
sprigs of fresh coriander, to
   garnish

To serve:
chargrilled courgettes
chargrilled tomatoes

Preheat oven to 200°C/400°F/Gas Mark 6, 15 minutes before cooking. Discard any skin from the monkfish tail and cut away and discard the central bone. Cut the fish into 4 equal-sized pieces and season to taste with salt and pepper and lay a bay leaf on each fillet, along with a slice of cheese.

Wrap each fillet with 2 slices of the Parma ham, so that the fish is covered completely. Tuck the ends of the Parma ham in and secure with a cocktail stick.

Lightly oil a baking sheet and place in the preheated oven for a few minutes. Place the fish on the preheated baking sheet, then place in the oven and cook for 12–15 minutes.

Bring a large saucepan of lightly salted water to the boil, then slowly add the pasta and cook for 5 minutes until *al dente*, or according to packet directions. Drain, reserving 2 tablespoons of the pasta-cooking liquor. Return the pasta to the saucepan and add the reserved pasta liquor, butter, lemon zest and juice. Toss until the pasta is well coated and glistening.

Twirl the pasta into small nests on 4 warmed serving plates and top with the monkfish parcels. Garnish with sprigs of coriander and serve with chargrilled courgettes and tomatoes.

Try This: FOR AN ALTERNATIVE: 114   FOR PUDDING: 352

Grilled Snapper with Roasted Pepper

SERVES 4

1 medium red pepper
1 medium green pepper
4–8 snapper fillets,
   depending on size, about
   450 g/1 lb

sea salt and freshly ground
   black pepper
1 tbsp olive oil
5 tbsp double cream
125 ml/4 fl oz white wine

1 tbsp freshly chopped dill
sprigs of fresh dill, to
   garnish
freshly cooked tagliatelle, to
   serve

Preheat the grill to a high heat and line the grill rack with tinfoil. Cut the tops off the peppers and divide into quarters. Remove the seeds and the membrane, then place on the foil-lined grill rack and cook for 8–10 minutes, turning frequently, until the skins have become charred and blackened. Remove from the grill rack, place in a polythene bag and leave until cool. When the peppers are cool, strip off the skin, slice thinly and reserve.

Cover the grill rack with another piece of tinfoil, then place the snapper fillets skin-side up on the grill rack. Season to taste with salt and pepper and brush with a little of the olive oil. Cook for 10-12 minutes, turning over once and brushing again with a little olive oil.

Pour the cream and wine into a small saucepan, bring to the boil and simmer for about 5 minutes until the sauce has thickened slightly. Add the dill, season to taste and stir in the sliced peppers. Arrange the cooked snapper fillets on warm serving plates and pour over the cream and pepper sauce. Garnish with sprigs of dill and serve immediately with freshly cooked tagliatelle.

 Try This: FOR AN ALTERNATIVE: 152   FOR PUDDING: 310

Supreme Baked Potatoes

SERVES 4

4 large baking potatoes
40 g/1½ oz butter
1 tbsp sunflower oil
1 carrot, peeled and
   chopped

2 celery stalks, trimmed and
   finely chopped
200 g can white crab meat
2 spring onions, trimmed
   and finely chopped

salt and freshly ground black
   pepper
50 g/2 oz Cheddar cheese,
   grated
tomato salad, to serve

Preheat the oven to 200°C/400°F/Gas Mark 6. Scrub the potatoes and prick all over with a fork, or thread 2 potatoes on to 2 long metal skewers. Place the potatoes in the preheated oven for 1–1½ hours, or until soft to the touch. Allow to cool a little, then cut in half.

Scoop out the cooked potato and turn into a bowl, leaving a reasonably firm potato shell. Mash the cooked potato flesh, then mix in the butter and mash until the butter has melted.

While the potatoes are cooking, heat the oil in a frying pan and cook the carrot and celery for 2 minutes. Cover the pan tightly and continue to cook for another 5 minutes, or until the vegetables are tender.

Add the cooked vegetables to the bowl of mashed potato and mix well. Fold in the crab meat and the spring onions, then season to taste with salt and pepper.

Pile the mixture back into the potato shells and press in firmly. Sprinkle the grated cheese over the top and return the potato halves to the oven for 12–15 minutes until hot, golden and bubbling. Serve immediately with a tomato salad.

Try This: FOR AN ALTERNATIVE: 150 FOR PUDDING: 374

Cheesy Vegetable & Prawn Bake

SERVES 4

175 g/6 oz long-grain rice
1 garlic clove, peeled and crushed
1 large egg, beaten
3 tbsp freshly shredded basil
4 tbsp Parmesan cheese, grated

salt and freshly ground black pepper
125 g/4 oz baby asparagus spears, trimmed
150 g/5 oz baby carrots, trimmed
150 g/5 oz fine green

beans, trimmed
150 g/5 oz cherry tomatoes
175 g/6 oz peeled prawns, thawed if frozen
125 g/4 oz mozzarella cheese, thinly sliced

Preheat the oven to 200°C/400°F/Gas Mark 6, about 10 minutes before required. Cook the rice in lightly salted boiling water for 12–15 minutes, or until tender, drain. Stir in the garlic, beaten egg, shredded basil, 2 tablespoons of the Parmesan cheese and season to taste with salt and pepper. Press this mixture into a greased 23 cm/9 inch square ovenproof dish and reserve.

Bring a large saucepan of water to the boil, then drop in the asparagus, carrots and green beans. Return to the boil and cook for 3–4 minutes. Drain and leave to cool.

Quarter or halve the cherry tomatoes and mix them into the cooled vegetables. Spread the prepared vegetables over the rice and top with the prawns. Season to taste with salt and pepper.

Cover the prawns with the mozzarella and sprinkle over the remaining Parmesan cheese. Bake in the preheated oven for 20–25 minutes until piping hot and golden brown in places. Serve immediately.

Try This: FOR AN ALTERNATIVE: 118 FOR PUDDING: 296

Pea & Prawn Risotto

SERVES 6

450 g/1 lb whole raw prawns
125 g/4 oz butter
1 red onion, peeled and
  chopped
4 garlic cloves, peeled and

finely chopped
225 g/8 oz Arborio rice
150 ml/¼ pint dry white wine
1.1 litres/2 pints vegetable or
  fish stock

375 g/13 oz frozen peas
4 tbsp freshly chopped mint
salt and freshly ground black
  pepper

Peel the prawns and reserve the heads and shells. Remove the black vein from the back of each prawn, then wash and dry on absorbent kitchen paper. Melt half the butter in a large frying pan, add the prawns' heads and shells and fry, stirring occasionally for 3–4 minutes, or until golden. Strain the butter, discard the heads and shells and return the butter to the pan.

Add a further 25 g/1 oz of butter to the pan and fry the onion and garlic for 5 minutes until softened, but not coloured. Add the rice and stir the grains in the butter for 1 minute, until they are coated thoroughly. Add the white wine and boil rapidly until the wine is reduced by half.

Bring the stock to a gentle simmer, and add to the rice, a ladleful at a time. Stir constantly, adding the stock as it is absorbed, until the rice is creamy, but still has a bite in the centre.

Melt the remaining butter and stir-fry the prawns for 3–4 minutes. Stir into the rice, along with all the pan juices and the peas. Add the chopped mint and season to taste with salt and pepper. Cover the pan and leave the prawns to infuse for 5 minutes before serving.

Try This: FOR AN ALTERNATIVE: 158 FOR PUDDING: 332

Meat

Pork Sausages with Onion Gravy & Best–ever Mash

SERVES 4

50 g/2 oz butter
1 tbsp olive oil
2 large onions, peeled and
    thinly sliced
pinch of sugar
1 tbsp freshly chopped thyme

1 tbsp plain flour
100 ml/3½ fl oz Madeira
200 ml/7 fl oz vegetable stock
8–12 good-quality butchers
    pork sausages, depending
    on size

For the mash:
900 g/2 lb floury potatoes,
    peeled
75 g/3 oz butter
4 tbsp crème fraîche or
    soured cream
salt and freshly ground black
    pepper

Melt the butter with the oil and add the onions. Cover and cook gently for about 20 minutes until the onions have collapsed. Add the sugar and stir well. Uncover and continue to cook, stirring often, until the onions are very soft and golden. Add the thyme, stir well, then add the flour, stirring. Gradually add the Madeira and the stock. Bring to the boil and simmer gently for 10 minutes.

Meanwhile, put the sausages in a large frying pan and cook over a medium heat for about 15–20 minutes, turning often, until golden brown and slightly sticky all over.

For the mash, boil the potatoes in plenty of lightly salted water for 15–18 minutes until tender. Drain well and return to the saucepan. Put the saucepan over a low heat to allow the potatoes to dry thoroughly. Remove from the heat and add the butter, and crème fraîche and season with salt and pepper. Mash thoroughly. Serve the potato mash topped with the sausages and onion gravy.

Try This: FOR AN ALTERNATIVE: 166   FOR PUDDING: 300

Oven–baked Pork Balls with Peppers

SERVES 4

For the garlic bread:
2–4 garlic cloves, peeled
50 g/2 oz butter, softened
1 tbsp freshly chopped parsley
2–3 tsp lemon juice
1 focaccia loaf

For the pork balls:
450 g/1 lb fresh pork mince
4 tbsp freshly chopped basil

2 garlic cloves, peeled and
   chopped
3 sun-dried tomatoes,
   chopped
salt and freshly ground black
   pepper
3 tbsp olive oil
1 medium red pepper,
   deseeded and cut into
   chunks

1 medium green pepper,
   deseeded and cut into
   chunks
1 medium yellow pepper,
   deseeded and cut into
   chunks
225 g/8 oz cherry tomatoes
2 tbsp balsamic vinegar

Preheat oven to 200°C/400°F/Gas Mark 6, 15 minutes before cooking. Crush the garlic, then blend with the softened butter, the parsley and enough lemon juice to give a soft consistency. Shape into a roll, wrap in baking parchment paper and chill in the refrigerator for at least 30 minutes.

Mix together the pork, basil, 1 chopped garlic clove, sun-dried tomatoes and seasoning until well combined. With damp hands, divide the mixture into 16, roll into balls and reserve.

Spoon the olive oil in a large roasting tin and place in the preheated oven for about 3 minutes, until very hot. Remove from the heat and stir in the pork balls, the remaining chopped garlic and peppers. Bake for about 15 minutes. Remove from the oven and stir in the cherry tomatoes and season to taste with plenty of salt and pepper. Bake for about a further 20 minutes.

Just before the pork balls are ready, slice the bread, toast lightly and spread with the prepared garlic butter. Remove the pork balls from the oven, stir in the vinegar and serve immediately with garlic bread.

Try This: FOR AN ALTERNATIVE: 164 FOR PUDDING: 324

Pork Chop Hotpot

SERVES 4

4 pork chops
flour for dusting
225 g/8 oz shallots, peeled
2 garlic cloves, peeled
50 g/2 oz sun-dried tomatoes
2 tbsp olive oil
400 g can plum tomatoes

150 ml/¼ pint red wine
150 ml/¼ pint chicken stock
3 tbsp tomato purée
2 tbsp freshly chopped
  oregano
salt and freshly ground black
  pepper

fresh oregano leaves, to
  garnish

To serve:
freshly cooked new potatoes
French beans

Preheat oven to 190°C/375°F/Gas Mark 5, 10 minutes before cooking. Trim the pork chops, removing any excess fat, wipe with a clean, damp cloth, then dust with a little flour and reserve. Cut the shallots in half if large. Chop the garlic and slice the sun-dried tomatoes.

Heat the olive oil in a large casserole dish and cook the pork chops for about 5 minutes, turning occasionally during cooking, until browned all over. Using a slotted spoon, carefully lift out of the dish and reserve. Add the shallots and cook for 5 minutes, stirring occasionally.

Return the pork chops to the casserole dish and scatter with the garlic and sun-dried tomatoes, then pour over the can of tomatoes with their juice.

Blend the red wine, stock and tomato purée together and add the chopped oregano. Season to taste with salt and pepper, then pour over the pork chops and bring to a gentle boil. Cover with a close-fitting lid and cook in the preheated oven for 1 hour, or until the pork chops are tender. Adjust the seasoning to taste, then scatter with a few oregano leaves and serve immediately with freshly cooked potatoes and French beans.

 Try This: FOR AN ALTERNATIVE: 170   FOR PUDDING: 358

Roast Cured Pork Loin with Baked Sliced Potatoes

SERVES 4

2 tbsp wholegrain mustard
2 tbsp clear honey
1 tsp coarsely crushed black pepper
900 g/2 lb piece smoked cured pork loin

900 g/2 lb potatoes, peeled and thinly sliced
75 g/3 oz butter, diced
1 large onion, peeled and finely chopped
25 g/1 oz plain flour

salt and freshly ground black pepper
600 ml/1 pint milk
fresh green salad, to serve

Preheat the oven to 190˚C/375˚F/Gas Mark 5. Mix together the mustard, honey and black pepper. Spread evenly over the pork loin. Place in the centre of a large square of tinfoil and wrap loosely. Cook in the preheated oven for 15 minutes per 450 g/1 lb, plus an extra 15 minutes (45 minutes), unwrapping the joint for the last 30 minutes cooking time.

Meanwhile, layer one-third of the potatoes, one-third of the butter, half the onions and half the flour in a large gratin dish. Add half the remaining potatoes and and half the remaining butter butter and the rest of the onions and flour. Finally, cover with the remaining potatoes. Season well with salt and pepper between layers. Pour in the milk and dot with the remaining butter. Cover the dish loosely with tinfoil and put in the oven below the pork. Cook for 1½ hours.

Remove the tinfoil from the potatoes and cook for a further 20 minutes until tender and golden. Remove the pork loin from the oven and leave to rest for 10 minutes before carving thinly. Serve with the potatoes and a fresh green salad.

Try This: FOR AN ALTERNATIVE: 172 FOR PUDDING: 332

Pork Loin Stuffed with Orange & Hazelnut Rice

SERVES 4

15 g/½ oz butter
1 shallot, peeled and finely chopped
50 g/2 oz long-grain brown rice
175 ml/6 fl oz vegetable stock
½ orange
25 g/1 oz ready-to-eat dried

prunes, stoned and chopped
25 g/1 oz hazelnuts, roasted and roughly chopped
1 small egg, beaten
1 tbsp freshly chopped parsley
salt and freshly ground pepper

450 g/1 lb boneless pork tenderloin or fillet, trimmed

To serve:
steamed courgettes
carrots

Preheat the oven to 190°C/375°F/Gas Mark 5, 10 minutes before required. Heat the butter in a small saucepan, add the shallot and cook gently for 2–3 minutes until softened. Add the rice and stir well for 1 minute. Add the stock, stir well and bring to the boil. Cover tightly and simmer gently for 30 minutes until the rice is tender and all the liquid is absorbed. Leave to cool.

Grate the orange rind and reserve. Remove the white pith and chop the orange flesh finely. Mix together the orange rind and flesh, prunes, hazelnuts, cooled rice, egg and parsley. Season to taste with salt and pepper.

Cut the fillet in half, then using a sharp knife, split the pork fillet lengthways almost in two, forming a pocket, leaving it just attached. Open out the pork and put between 2 pieces of clingfilm. Flatten using a meat mallet until about half its original thickness. Spoon the filling into the pocket and close the fillet over. Tie along the length with kitchen string at regular intervals.

Put the pork fillet in a small roasting tray and cook in the top of the preheated oven for 25–30 minutes, or until the meat is just tender. Remove from the oven and allow to rest for 5 minutes. Slice into rounds and serve with steamed courgettes and carrots.

Try This: FOR AN ALTERNATIVE: 170   FOR PUDDING: 360

Pork Cabbage Parcels

SERVES 4

8 large green cabbage
leaves
1 tbsp vegetable oil
2 celery sticks, trimmed and
chopped
1 carrot, peeled and cut into
matchsticks
125 g/4 oz fresh pork mince
50 g/2 oz button

mushrooms, wiped and
sliced
1 tsp Chinese five spice
powder
50 g/2 oz cooked long-grain
rice
juice of 1 lemon
1 tbsp soy sauce
150 ml/¼ pint chicken stock

For the tomato sauce:
1 tbsp vegetable oil
1 bunch spring onions,
trimmed and chopped
400 g can chopped tomatoes
1 tbsp light soy sauce
1 tbsp freshly chopped mint
freshly ground black pepper

Preheat the oven to 180˚C/350˚F/Gas Mark 4, 10 minutes before cooking. To make the
sauce, heat the oil in a heavy-based saucepan, add the spring onions and cook for 2 minutes
or until softened.

Add the tomatoes, soy sauce and mint to the saucepan, bring to the boil, cover, then simmer
for 10 minutes. Season to taste with pepper. Reheat when required.

Meanwhile, blanch the cabbage leaves in a large saucepan of lightly salted water for 3 minutes.
Drain and refresh under cold running water. Pat dry with absorbent kitchen paper and reserve.

Heat the oil in a small saucepan, add the celery, carrot and pork mince and cook for 3
minutes. Add the mushrooms and cook for 3 minutes. Stir in the Chinese five spice powder,
rice, lemon juice and soy sauce and heat through.

Place some of the filling in the centre of each cabbage leaf and fold to enclose the filling.
Place in a shallow ovenproof dish seam-side down. Pour over the stock and cook in the
preheated oven for 30 minutes. Serve immediately with the reheated tomato sauce.

Try This: FOR AN ALTERNATIVE: 194   FOR PUDDING: 378

Leek & Ham Risotto

SERVES 4

1 tbsp olive oil
25 g/1 oz butter
1 medium onion, peeled and finely chopped
4 leeks, trimmed and thinly sliced

1½ tbsp freshly chopped thyme
350 g/12 oz Arborio rice
1.4 litres/2¼ pints vegetable or chicken stock, heated
225 g/8 oz cooked ham

175 g/6 oz peas, thawed if frozen
50 g/2 oz Parmesan cheese, grated
salt and freshly ground black pepper

Heat the oil and half the butter together in a large saucepan. Add the onion and leeks and cook over a medium heat for 6–8 minutes, stirring occasionally, until soft and beginning to colour. Stir in the thyme and cook briefly.

Add the rice and stir well. Continue stirring over a medium heat for about 1 minute until the rice is glossy. Add a ladleful or two of the stock and stir well until the stock is absorbed. Continue adding stock, a ladleful at a time, and stirring well between additions, until about two-thirds of the stock has been added.

Meanwhile, either chop or finely shred the ham, then add to the saucepan of rice together with the peas. Continue adding ladlefuls of stock, as described in step 2, until the rice is tender and the ham is heated through.

Add the remaining butter, sprinkle over the Parmesan cheese and season to taste with salt and pepper. When the butter has melted and the cheese has softened, stir well to incorporate. Taste and adjust the seasoning, then serve immediately.

Try This: FOR AN ALTERNATIVE: 242   FOR PUDDING: 364

Lancashire Hotpot

SERVES 4

1 kg/2¼ lb middle end neck
of lamb, divided into
cutlets
2 tbsp vegetable oil
2 large onions, peeled and
sliced
2 tsp plain flour

150 ml/¼ pint vegetable or
lamb stock
700 g/1½ lb waxy potatoes,
peeled and thickly sliced
salt and freshly ground black
pepper
1 bay leaf

2 sprigs of fresh thyme
1 tbsp melted butter
2 tbsp freshly chopped
herbs, to garnish
freshly cooked green beans,
to serve

Preheat the oven to 170˚C/325˚F/Gas Mark 3. Trim any excess fat from the lamb cutlets.
Heat the oil in a frying pan and brown the cutlets in batches for 3–4 minutes. Remove with a
slotted spoon and reserve. Add the onions to the frying pan and cook for 6–8 minutes until
softened and just beginning to colour, then remove and reserve.

Stir in the flour and cook for a few seconds, then gradually pour in the stock, stirring well, and
bring to the boil. Remove from the heat.

Spread the base of a large casserole with half the potato slices. Top with half the onions and
season well with salt and pepper. Arrange the browned meat in a layer. Season again and add
the remaining onions, bay leaf and thyme. Pour in the remaining liquid from the onions and top
with remaining potatoes so that they overlap in a single layer. Brush the potatoes with the
melted butter and season again.

Cover the saucepan and cook in the preheated oven for 2 hours, uncovering for the last 30
minutes to allow the potatoes to brown. Garnish with chopped herbs and serve immediately
with green beans.

Try This: FOR AN ALTERNATIVE: 180 FOR PUDDING: 330

Shepherd's Pie

SERVES 4

2 tbsp vegetable or olive oil
1 onion, peeled and finely chopped
1 carrot, peeled and finely chopped
1 celery stalk, trimmed and finely chopped
1 tbsp sprigs of fresh thyme

450 g/1 lb leftover roast lamb, finely chopped
150 ml/¼ pint red wine
150 ml/¼ pint lamb or vegetable stock or leftover gravy
2 tbsp tomato purée
salt and freshly ground

black pepper
700 g/1½ lb potatoes, peeled and cut into chunks
25 g/1 oz butter
6 tbsp milk
1 tbsp freshly chopped parsley
fresh herbs, to garnish

Preheat the oven to 200°C/400°F/Gas Mark 6, about 15 minutes before cooking. Heat the oil in a large saucepan and add the onion, carrot and celery. Cook over a medium heat for 8–10 minutes until softened and starting to brown.

Add the thyme and cook briefly, then add the cooked lamb, wine, stock and tomato purée. Season to taste with salt and pepper and simmer gently for 25–30 minutes until reduced and thickened. Remove from the heat to cool slightly and season again.

Meanwhile, boil the potatoes in plenty of salted water for 12–15 minutes until tender. Drain and return to the saucepan over a low heat to dry out. Remove from the heat and add the butter, milk and parsley. Mash until creamy, adding a little more milk, if necessary. Adjust the seasoning.

Transfer the lamb mixture to a shallow ovenproof dish. Spoon the mash over the filling and spread evenly to cover completely. Fork the surface, place on a baking sheet, then cook in the preheated oven for 25–30 minutes until the potato topping is browned and the filling is piping hot. Garnish and serve.

 Try This: FOR AN ALTERNATIVE: 178   FOR PUDDING: 344

Roast Leg of Lamb & Boulangere Potatoes

SERVES 6

1.1 kg/2½ lb potatoes, peeled
1 large onion, peeled and finely sliced
salt and freshly ground black pepper
2 tbsp olive oil

50 g/2 oz butter
200 ml/7 fl oz lamb stock
100 ml/3½ fl oz milk
2 kg/4½ lb leg of lamb
2–3 sprigs of fresh rosemary
6 large garlic cloves, peeled

and finely sliced
6 anchovy fillets, drained
extra sprigs of fresh rosemary, to garnish

Preheat the oven to 230°C/450°F/Gas Mark 8. Finely slice the potatoes – a mandolin is the best tool for this. Layer the potatoes with the onion in a large roasting tin, seasoning each layer with salt and pepper. Drizzle about 1 tablespoon of the olive oil over the potatoes and add the butter in small pieces. Pour in the lamb stock and milk. Set aside.

Make small incisions all over the lamb with the point of a small, sharp knife. Into each incision insert a small piece of rosemary, a sliver of garlic and a piece of anchovy fillet.

Drizzle the leg of lamb and its flavourings with the rest of the olive oil and season well. Place the meat directly onto a shelf in the preheated oven. Position the roasting tin of potatoes directly underneath to catch the juices during cooking. Roast for 15 minutes per 500 g/1 lb 2 oz (about 1 hour for a joint this size), reducing the oven temperature after 20 minutes to 200°C/400°F/Gas Mark 6.

When the lamb is cooked, remove from the oven and allow to rest for 10 minutes before carving. Meanwhile, increase the oven heat and cook the potatoes for a further 10–15 minutes to crisp up. Garnish with fresh rosemary sprigs and serve immediately with the lamb.

Try This: FOR AN ALTERNATIVE: 186   FOR PUDDING: 296

Leg of Lamb with Minted Rice

SERVES 4

1 tbsp olive oil
1 medium onion, peeled
  and finely chopped
1 garlic clove, peeled
  and crushed
1 celery stalk, trimmed

and chopped
1 large mild red chilli,
  deseeded and chopped
75 g/3 oz long-grain rice
150 ml/¼ pint lamb or
  chicken stock

2 tbsp freshly chopped mint
salt and freshly ground black
  pepper
1.4 kg/3 lb boned leg of lamb
freshly cooked vegetables,
  to serve

Preheat the oven to 190°C/375°F/Gas Mark 5, 10 minutes before roasting. Heat the oil in a frying pan and gently cook the onion for 5 minutes. Stir in the garlic, celery and chilli and continue to cook for 3–4 minutes.

Place the rice and the stock in a large saucepan and cook, covered, for 10–12 minutes or until the rice is tender and all the liquid is absorbed. Stir in the onion and celery mixture, then leave to cool. Once the rice mixture is cold, stir in the chopped mint and season to taste with salt and pepper.

Place the boned lamb skin-side down and spoon the rice mixture along the centre of the meat. Roll up the meat to enclose the stuffing and tie securely with string. Place in a roasting tin and roast in the preheated oven for 1 hour 20 minutes, or until cooked to personal preference. Remove from the oven and leave to rest in a warm place for 20 minutes, before carving. Serve with a selection of cooked vegetables.

Try This: FOR AN ALTERNATIVE: 188   FOR PUDDING: 298

Roasted Lamb
with Rosemary & Garlic

SERVES 6

1.6 kg/3½ lb leg of lamb
8 garlic cloves, peeled
salt and freshly ground black
    pepper
few sprigs of fresh rosemary

4 slices pancetta
4 tbsp olive oil
4 tbsp red wine vinegar
900 g/2 lb potatoes
1 large onion

sprigs of fresh rosemary,
    to garnish
freshly cooked ratatouille,
    to serve

Preheat oven to 200°C/400°F/Gas Mark 6, 15 minutes before roasting. Wipe the leg of lamb with a clean damp cloth, then place the lamb in a large roasting tin. With a sharp knife, make small, deep incisions into the meat. Cut 2–3 garlic cloves into small slivers, then insert with a few small sprigs of rosemary into the lamb. Season to taste with salt and pepper and cover the lamb with the slices of pancetta.

Drizzle over 1 tablespoon of the olive oil and lay a few more rosemary sprigs across the lamb. Roast in the preheated oven for 30 minutes, then pour over the vinegar.

Peel the potatoes and cut into large dice. Peel the onion and cut into thick wedges then thickly slice the remaining garlic. Arrange around the lamb. Pour the remaining olive oil over the potatoes, then reduce the oven temperature to 180°C/350°F/Gas Mark 4 and roast for a further 1 hour, or until the lamb is tender. Garnish with fresh sprigs of rosemary and serve immediately with the roast potatoes and ratatouille.

Try This: FOR AN ALTERNATIVE: 182   FOR PUDDING: 306

Crown Roast of Lamb

SERVES 6

1 lamb crown roast
salt and freshly ground black
  pepper
1 tbsp sunflower oil
1 small onion, peeled and
  finely chopped
2–3 garlic cloves, peeled and
  crushed

2 celery stalks, trimmed and
  finely chopped
125 g/4 oz cooked mixed
  basmati and wild rice
75 g/3 oz ready-to-eat-dried
  apricots, chopped
50 g/2 oz pine nuts, toasted
1 tbsp finely grated

  orange rind
2 tbsp freshly chopped
  coriander
1 small egg, beaten
freshly roasted potatoes and
  green vegetables, to
  serve:

Preheat the oven to 180°C/350°F/Gas Mark 4, about 10 minutes before roasting. Wipe the crown roast and season the cavity with salt and pepper. Place in a roasting tin and cover the ends of the bones with small pieces of tinfoil.

Heat the oil in a small saucepan and cook the onion, garlic and celery for 5 minutes, then remove the saucepan from the heat. Add the cooked rice with the apricots, pine nuts, orange rind and coriander. Season with salt and pepper, then stir in the egg and mix well.

Carefully spoon the prepared stuffing into the cavity of the lamb, then roast in the preheated oven for 1–1½ hours. Remove the lamb from the oven and remove and discard the tinfoil from the bones. Return to the oven and continue to cook for a further 15 minutes, or until cooked to personal preference.

Remove from the oven and leave to rest for 10 minutes before serving with the roast potatoes and freshly cooked vegetables.

Try This: FOR AN ALTERNATIVE: 184   FOR PUDDING: 302

Red Wine Risotto with Lambs' Kidneys & Caramelised Shallots

SERVES 4

8 lambs' kidneys, halved and cores removed
150 ml/¼ pint milk
2 tbsp olive oil
50 g/2 oz butter
275 g/10 oz shallots, peeled and halved if large

1 onion, peeled and finely chopped
2 garlic cloves, peeled and finely chopped
350 g/12 oz Arborio rice
225 ml/8 fl oz red wine
1 litre/1¾ pints chicken or

vegetable stock, heated
1 tbsp sprigs of fresh thyme
50 g/2 oz Parmesan cheese, grated
salt and freshly ground black pepper
fresh herbs, to garnish

Place the lambs' kidneys in a bowl and pour the milk over. Leave to soak for 15–20 minutes, then drain and pat dry on absorbent kitchen paper. Discard the milk.

Heat 1 tablespoon of the oil with 25 g/1 oz of the butter in a medium saucepan. Add the shallots, cover and cook for 10 minutes over a gentle heat. Remove the lid and cook for a further 10 minutes, or until tender and golden.

Meanwhile, heat the remaining oil with the remaining butter in a deep-sided frying pan. Add the onion and cook over a medium heat for 5–7 minutes until starting to brown. Add the garlic and cook briefly. Stir in the rice and cook for a further minute until glossy and well coated in oil and butter. Add half the red wine and stir until absorbed. Add a ladleful or two of the stock and stir well until the stock is absorbed. Continue adding the stock, a ladleful at a time, and stirring well between additions, until all of the stock is added and the rice is just tender, but still firm. Remove from the heat.

Meanwhile, when the rice is nearly cooked, increase the heat under the shallots, add the thyme and kidneys. Cook for 3–4 minutes, then add the remaining wine. Bring to the boil, then simmer rapidly until the red wine is reduced and syrupy. Stir the cheese into the rice with the caramelised shallots and kidneys. Season to taste, garnish and serve.

Try This: FOR AN ALTERNATIVE: 242   FOR PUDDING: 320

Marinated Lamb Chops with Garlic Fried Potatoes

SERVES 4

4 thick lamb chump chops
3 tbsp olive oil
550 g/1¼ lb potatoes, peeled and cut into 1 cm/½ inch dice
6 unpeeled garlic cloves
mixed salad or freshly

cooked vegetables, to serve

For the marinade:
1 small bunch of fresh thyme, leaves removed
1 tbsp freshly chopped

rosemary
1 tsp salt
2 garlic cloves, peeled and crushed
rind and juice of 1 lemon
2 tbsp olive oil

Trim the chops of any excess fat, wipe with a clean damp cloth and reserve. To make the marinade, using a pestle and mortar, pound the thyme leaves and rosemary with the salt until pulpy. Add the garlic and continue pounding until crushed. Stir in the lemon rind and juice and the olive oil.

Pour the marinade over the lamb chops, turning them until they are well coated. Cover lightly and leave to marinate in the refrigerator for about 1 hour.

Meanwhile, heat the oil in a large non-stick frying pan. Add the potatoes and garlic and cook over a low heat for about 20 minutes, stirring occasionally. Increase the heat and cook for a further 10–15 minutes until golden. Drain on absorbent kitchen paper and add salt to taste. Keep warm.

Heat a griddle pan until almost smoking. Add the lamb chops and cook for 3–4 minutes on each side until golden, but still pink in the middle. Serve with the potatoes, and either a mixed salad or freshly cooked vegetables.

Lamb Meatballs with Savoy Cabbage

SERVES 4

450 g/1 lb fresh lamb mince
1 tbsp freshly chopped
    parsley
1 tbsp freshly grated root
    ginger
1 tbsp light soy sauce
1 medium egg yolk

4 tbsp dark soy sauce
2 tbsp dry sherry
1 tbsp cornflour
3 tbsp vegetable oil
2 garlic cloves, peeled and
    chopped
1 bunch spring onions,

trimmed and shredded
½ Savoy cabbage, trimmed
    and shredded
½ head Chinese leaves,
    trimmed and shredded
freshly chopped red chilli, to
    garnish

Place the lamb mince in a large bowl with the parsley, ginger, light soy sauce and egg yolk and mix together. Divide the mixture into walnut-sized pieces and using your hands roll into balls. Place on a baking sheet, cover with clingfilm and chill in the refrigerator for at least 30 minutes.

Meanwhile, mix together the dark soy sauce, sherry and cornflour with 2 tablespoons of water in a small bowl until smooth. Reserve.

Heat a wok, add the oil and when hot, add the meatballs and cook for 5–8 minutes, or until browned all over, turning occasionally. Using a slotted spoon, transfer the meatballs to a large plate and keep warm.

Add the garlic, spring onions, Savoy cabbage and the Chinese leaves to the wok and stir-fry for 3 minutes. Pour over the reserved soy sauce mixture, bring to the boil, then simmer for 30 seconds or until thickened. Return the meatballs to the wok and mix in. Garnish with chopped red chilli and serve immediately.

Try This: FOR AN ALTERNATIVE: 174   FOR PUDDING: 332

Brandied Lamb Chops

SERVES 4

8 lamb loin chops
3 tbsp groundnut oil
5 cm/2 inch piece fresh root ginger, peeled and cut into matchsticks
2 garlic cloves, peeled and chopped
225 g/8 oz button

mushrooms, wiped and halved if large
2 tbsp light soy sauce
2 tbsp dry sherry
1 tbsp brandy
1 tsp Chinese five spice powder
1 tsp soft brown sugar

200 ml/7 fl oz lamb or chicken stock
1 tsp sesame oil

To serve:
freshly cooked rice
freshly stir-fried vegetables

Using a sharp knife, trim the lamb chops, discarding any sinew or fat. Heat a wok or large frying pan, add the oil and when hot, add the lamb chops and cook for 3 minutes on each side or until browned. Using a fish slice, transfer the lamb chops to a plate and keep warm.

Add the ginger, garlic and button mushrooms to the wok and stir-fry for 3 minutes or until the mushrooms have browned.

Return the lamb chops to the wok together with the soy sauce, sherry, brandy, five spice powder and sugar. Pour in the stock, bring to the boil, then reduce the heat slightly and simmer for 4–5 minutes, or until the lamb is tender, ensuring that the liquid does not evaporate completely. Add the sesame oil and heat for a further 30 seconds. Turn into a warmed serving dish and serve immediately with freshly cooked rice and stir-fried vegetables.

Try This: FOR AN ALTERNATIVE: 222   FOR PUDDING: 312

Seared Calves' Liver with Onions & Mustard Mash

SERVES 2

2 tbsp olive oil
100 g/3½ oz butter
3 large onions, peeled and
  finely sliced
pinch of sugar
salt and freshly ground

black pepper
1 tbsp sprigs of fresh thyme
1 tbsp balsamic vinegar
700 g/1½ lb potatoes, peeled
  and cut into chunks
6–8 tbsp milk

2 tbsp wholegrain mustard
3–4 fresh sage leaves
550 g/1¼ lb thinly sliced
  calves' liver
1 tsp lemon juice

Preheat the oven to 150°C/300°F/Gas Mark 2. Heat half the oil and 25 g/1 oz of the butter in a flameproof casserole. When foaming, add the onions. Cover and cook over a low heat for 20 minutes until softened and beginning to collapse. Add the sugar and season with salt and pepper. Stir in the thyme. Cover the casserole and transfer to the preheated oven. Cook for a further 30–45 minutes until softened completely, but not browned. Remove from the oven and stir in the balsamic vinegar.

Meanwhile, boil the potatoes in boiling salted water for 15–18 minutes until tender. Drain well, then return to the pan. Place over a low heat to dry completely, remove from the heat and stir in 50 g/2 oz of the butter, the milk, 1 tbsp of mustard and salt and pepper to taste. Mash thoroughly until creamy and keep warm.

Heat a large frying pan and add the remaining butter and oil. When it is foaming, add the remaining mustard and sage leaves and stir for a few seconds, then add the liver. Cook over a high heat for 1–2 minutes on each side. It should remain slightly pink: do not overcook. Remove the liver from the pan. Add the lemon juice to the pan and swirl around to deglaze.

To serve, place a large spoonful of the mashed potato on each plate. Top with some of the melting onions, the liver and finally the pan juices.

Spaghetti Bolognese

SERVES 4

1 carrot
2 celery stalks
1 onion
2 garlic cloves
450 g/1 lb lean minced beef
  steak
225 g/8 oz smoked streaky

bacon, chopped
1 tbsp plain flour
150 ml/¼ pint red wine
379 g can chopped tomatoes
2 tbsp tomato purée
2 tsp dried mixed herbs
salt and freshly ground

black pepper
pinch of sugar
350 g/12 oz spaghetti
sprigs of fresh oregano, to
  garnish
shavings of Parmesan
  cheese, to serve

Peel and chop the carrot, trim and chop the celery, then peel and chop the onion and garlic. Heat a large non-stick frying pan and sauté the minced beef and bacon for 5–10 minutes, stirring occasionally, until browned. Add the prepared vegetables to the frying pan and cook for about
3 minutes, or until softened, stirring occasionally.

Add the flour and cook for 1 minute. Stir in the red wine, tomatoes, tomato purée, mixed herbs, seasoning to taste and sugar. Bring to the boil, then cover and simmer for 45 minutes, stirring occasionally.

Meanwhile, bring a large saucepan of lightly salted water to the boil and cook the spaghetti for 10–12 minutes, or until *al dente*. Drain well and divide between 4 serving plates. Spoon over the sauce, garnish with a few sprigs of oregano and serve immediately with plenty of Parmesan shavings.

Try This: FOR AN ALTERNATIVE: 208 FOR PUDDING: 376

Traditional Lasagne

SERVES 4

450 g/1 lb lean minced beef
175 g/6 oz pancetta or smoked streaky bacon, chopped
1 large onion, peeled and chopped
2 celery stalks, trimmed and chopped
125 g/4 oz button mushrooms, wiped and chopped
2 garlic cloves, peeled and chopped

90 g/3½ oz plain flour
300 ml/½ pint beef stock
1 tbsp freeze-dried mixed herbs
5 tbsp tomato purée
salt and freshly ground black pepper
75 g/3 oz butter
1 tsp English mustard powder
pinch of freshly grated nutmeg
900 ml/1½ pints milk

125 g/4 oz Parmesan cheese, grated
125 g/4 oz Cheddar cheese, grated
8–12 precooked lasagne sheets

To serve:
crusty bread
fresh green salad leaves

Preheat oven to 200°C/400°F/Gas Mark 6, 15 minutes before cooking. Cook the minced beef and pancetta in a large saucepan for 10 minutes, stirring to break up any lumps. Add the onion, celery and mushrooms and cook for 4 minutes, or until softened slightly. Stir in the garlic and 1 tablespoon of the flour, then cook for 1 minute. Stir in the stock, herbs and tomato purée. Season to taste with salt and pepper. Bring to the boil, then cover, reduce the heat and simmer for 45 minutes.

Meanwhile, melt the butter in a small saucepan and stir in the remaining flour, mustard powder and nutmeg, until well blended. Cook for 2 minutes. Remove from the heat and gradually blend in the milk until smooth. Return to the heat and bring to the boil, stirring, until thickened. Gradually stir in half the Parmesan and Cheddar cheeses until melted. Season to taste.

Spoon half the meat mixture into the base of a large ovenproof dish. Top with a single layer of pasta. Spread over half the sauce and scatter with half the cheese. Repeat layers finishing with cheese. Bake in the preheated oven for 30 minutes, or until the pasta is cooked and the top is golden brown and bubbly. Serve immediately with crusty bread and a green salad.

 Try This: FOR AN ALTERNATIVE: 204   FOR PUDDING: 368

Cannelloni

SERVES 4

2 tbsp olive oil
175 g/6 oz fresh pork mince
75 g/3 oz chicken livers,
  chopped
1 small onion, peeled and
  chopped
1 garlic clove, peeled and
  chopped
175 g/6 oz frozen chopped

spinach, thawed
1 tbsp freeze-dried oregano
pinch of freshly grated
  nutmeg
salt and freshly ground black
  pepper
175 g/6 oz ricotta cheese
25 g/1 oz butter
25 g/1 oz plain flour

600 ml/1 pint milk
600 ml/1 pint ready-made
  tomato sauce
16 precooked cannelloni
  tubes
50 g/2 oz Parmesan cheese,
  grated
green salad, to serve

Preheat oven to 190°C/375°F/Gas Mark 5, 10 minutes before cooking. Heat the olive oil in a frying pan and cook the mince and chicken livers for about 5 minutes, stirring occasionally, until browned all over. Break up any lumps if necessary with a wooden spoon.

Add the onion and garlic and cook for 4 minutes, until softened. Add the spinach, oregano, nutmeg and season to taste with salt and pepper. Cook until all the liquid has evaporated, then remove the pan from the heat and allow to cool. Stir in the ricotta cheese.

Meanwhile, melt the butter in a small saucepan and stir in the plain flour to form a roux. Cook for 2 minutes, stirring occasionally. Remove from the heat and blend in the milk until smooth. Return to the heat and bring to the boil, stirring until the sauce has thickened. Reserve.

Spoon a thin layer of the tomato sauce on the base of a large ovenproof dish. Divide the pork filling between the cannelloni tubes. Arrange on top of the tomato sauce. Spoon over the remaining tomato sauce. Pour over the white sauce and sprinkle with the Parmesan cheese. Bake in the preheated oven for 30–35 minutes, or until the cannelloni is tender and the top is golden brown. Serve immediately with a green salad.

Try This: FOR AN ALTERNATIVE: 202   FOR PUDDING: 344

Italian Beef Pot Roast

SERVES 6

1.8 kg/4 lb brisket of beef
225 g/8 oz small onions, peeled
3 garlic cloves, peeled and chopped
2 celery sticks, trimmed and chopped

2 carrots, peeled and sliced
450 g/1 lb ripe tomatoes
300 ml/½ pint Italian red wine
2 tbsp olive oil
300 ml/½ pint beef stock
1 tbsp tomato purée
2 tsp freeze-dried mixed herbs

salt and freshly ground black pepper
25 g/1 oz butter
25 g/1 oz plain flour
freshly cooked vegetables, to serve

Preheat oven to 150°C/300°F/Gas Mark 2, 10 minutes before cooking. Place the beef in a bowl. Add the onions, garlic, celery and carrots. Place the tomatoes in a bowl and cover with boiling water. Allow to stand for 2 minutes and drain. Peel away the skins, discard the seeds and chop, then add to the bowl with the red wine. Cover tightly and marinate in the refrigerator overnight.

Lift the marinated beef from the bowl and pat dry with absorbent kitchen paper. Heat the olive oil in a large casserole dish and cook the beef until it is browned all over, then remove from the dish. Drain the vegetables from the marinade, reserving the marinade. Add the vegetables to the casserole dish and fry gently for 5 minutes, stirring occasionally, until all the vegetables are browned.

Return the beef to the casserole dish with the marinade, beef stock, tomato purée, mixed herbs and season with salt and pepper. Bring to the boil, then cover and cook in the preheated oven for 3 hours.

Using a slotted spoon transfer the beef and any large vegetables to a plate and leave in a warm place. Blend the butter and flour to form a paste. Bring the casserole juices to the boil and then gradually stir in small spoonfuls of the paste. Cook until thickened. Serve with the sauce and a selection of vegetables.

Try This: FOR AN ALTERNATIVE: 210   FOR PUDDING: 366

Spaghetti & Meatballs

SERVES 4

400 g can chopped tomatoes
1 tbsp tomato paste
1 tsp chilli sauce
¼ tsp brown sugar
salt and freshly ground black
  pepper
350 g/12 oz spaghetti
75g/3 oz Cheddar cheese,

grated, plus extra to serve
freshly chopped parsley, to
  garnish

For the meatballs:
450 g/1 lb lean pork or
  beef mince
125 g/4 oz fresh breadcrumbs

1 large onion, peeled and
  finely chopped
1 medium egg, beaten
1 tbsp tomato paste
2 tbsp freshly chopped
  parsley
1 tbsp freshly chopped
  oregano

Preheat the oven to 200°C/400°F/Gas Mark 6, 15 minutes before using. Place the chopped tomatoes, tomato paste, chilli sauce and sugar in a saucepan. Season to taste with salt and pepper and bring to the boil. Cover and simmer for 15 minutes, then cook, uncovered, for a further 10 minutes, or until the sauce has reduced and thickened.

Meanwhile, make the meatballs. Place the meat, breadcrumbs and onion in a food processor. Blend until all the ingredients are well mixed. Add the beaten egg, tomato paste, parsley and oregano and season to taste. Blend again.

Shape the mixture into small balls, about the size of an apricot, and place on an oiled baking tray. Cook in the preheated oven for 25–30 minutes, or until browned and cooked.

Meanwhile, bring a large pan of lightly salted water to a rolling boil. Add the pasta and cook according to the packet instructions, or until *al dente*.

Drain the pasta and return to the pan. Pour over the tomato sauce and toss gently to coat the spaghetti. Tip into a warmed serving dish and top with the meatballs. Garnish with chopped parsley and serve immediately with grated cheese.

Try This: FOR AN ALTERNATIVE: 200   FOR PUDDING: 368

Pan–fried Beef with Creamy Mushrooms

SERVES 4

225 g/8 oz shallots, peeled
2 garlic cloves, peeled
2 tbsp olive oil
4 medallions of beef
4 plum tomatoes

125 g/4 oz flat mushrooms
3 tbsp brandy
150 ml/¼ pint red wine
salt and freshly ground black
    pepper

4 tbsp double cream

To serve:
baby new potatoes
freshly cooked green beans

Cut the shallots in half if large, then chop the garlic. Heat the oil in a large frying pan and cook the shallots for about 8 minutes, stirring occasionally, until almost softened. Add the garlic and beef and cook for 8–10 minutes, turning once during cooking until the meat is browned all over. Using a slotted spoon, transfer the beef to a plate and keep warm.

Rinse the tomatoes and cut into eighths, then wipe the mushrooms and slice. Add to the pan and cook for 5 minutes, stirring frequently until the mushrooms have softened.

Pour in the brandy and heat through. Draw the pan off the heat and carefully ignite. Allow the flames to subside. Pour in the wine, return to the heat and bring to the boil. Boil until reduced by one-third. Draw the pan off the heat, season to taste with salt and pepper, add the cream and stir.

Arrange the beef on serving plates and spoon over the sauce. Serve with baby new potatoes and some green beans.

Try This: FOR AN ALTERNATIVE: 206   FOR PUDDING: 332

Grilled Steaks with Saffron Potatoes & Roast Tomatoes

SERVES 4

700 g/1½ lb new potatoes, halved
few strands of saffron
300 ml/½ pint vegetable or beef stock
1 small onion, peeled and finely chopped
75 g/3 oz butter
salt and freshly ground black pepper
2 tsp balsamic vinegar
2 tbsp olive oil
1 tsp caster sugar
8 plum tomatoes, halved
4 boneless sirloin steaks, each weighing 225 g/8 oz
2 tbsp freshly chopped parsley

Cook the potatoes in boiling salted water for 8 minutes and drain well. Return the potatoes to the saucepan along with the saffron, stock, onion and 25 g/1 oz of the butter. Season to taste with salt and pepper and simmer, uncovered for 10 minutes until the potatoes are tender.

Meanwhile, preheat the grill to medium. Mix together the vinegar, olive oil, sugar and seasoning. Arrange the tomatoes cut-side up in a foil-lined grill pan and drizzle over the dressing. Grill for 12–15 minutes, basting occasionally, until tender.

Melt the remaining butter in a frying pan. Add the steaks and cook for 4–8 minutes to taste and depending on thickness.

Arrange the potatoes and tomatoes in the centre of 4 serving plates. Top with the steaks along with any pan juices. Sprinkle over the parsley and serve immediately.

Try This: FOR AN ALTERNATIVE: 210   FOR PUDDING: 296

Chilli Con Carne with Crispy–skinned Potatoes

SERVES 4

2 tbsp vegetable oil, plus extra for brushing
1 large onion, peeled and finely chopped
1 garlic clove, peeled and finely chopped
1 red chilli, deseeded and finely chopped

450 g/1 lb chuck steak, finely chopped, or lean beef mince
1 tbsp chilli powder
400 g can chopped tomatoes
2 tbsp tomato purée
400 g can red kidney beans, drained and rinsed

4 large baking potatoes
coarse salt and freshly ground black pepper

To serve:
ready-made guacamole
soured cream

Preheat the oven to 150°C/300°F/Gas Mark 2. Heat the oil in a large flameproof casserole and add the onion. Cook gently for 10 minutes until soft and lightly browned. Add the garlic and chilli and cook briefly. Increase the heat. Add the chuck steak or lean mince and cook for a further 10 minutes, stirring occasionally, until browned.

Add the chilli powder and stir well. Cook for about 2 minutes, then add the chopped tomatoes and tomato purée. Bring slowly to the boil. Cover and cook in the preheated oven for 1½ hours. Remove from the oven and stir in the kidney beans. Return to the oven for a further 15 minutes.

Meanwhile, brush a little vegetable oil all over the potatoes and rub on some coarse salt. Put the potatoes in the oven alongside the chilli.

Remove the chilli and potatoes from the oven. Cut a cross in each potato, then squeeze to open slightly and season to taste with salt and pepper. Serve with the chilli, guacamole and soured cream.

Try This: FOR AN ALTERNATIVE: 60   FOR PUDDING: 310

Poultry

Slow Roast Chicken with Potatoes & Oregano

SERVES 6

1.4–1.8 kg/3–4 lb oven-ready chicken, preferably free range
1 lemon, halved
1 onion, peeled and quartered

50 g/2 oz butter, softened
salt and freshly ground black pepper
1 kg/2¼ lb potatoes, peeled and quartered
3–4 tbsp extra-virgin olive oil

1 tbsp dried oregano, crumbled
1 tsp fresh thyme leaves
2 tbsp freshly chopped thyme

Preheat the oven to 200°C/400°F/Gas Mark 6. Rinse the chicken and dry well, inside and out, with absorbent kitchen paper. Rub the chicken all over with the lemon halves, then squeeze the juice over it and into the cavity. Put the squeezed halves into the cavity with the quartered onion. Rub the softened butter all over the chicken and season to taste with salt and pepper, then put it in a large roasting tin, breast-side down.

Toss the potatoes in the oil, season with salt and pepper to taste and add the dried oregano and fresh thyme. Arrange the potatoes with the oil around the chicken and carefully pour 150 ml/¼ pint water into one end of the pan (not over the oil). Roast in the preheated oven for 25 minutes. Reduce the oven temperature to 190°C/375°F/Gas Mark 5 and turn the chicken breast-side up. Turn the potatoes, sprinkle over half the fresh herbs and baste the chicken and potatoes with the juices. Continue roasting for 1 hour, or until the chicken is cooked, basting occasionally. If the liquid evaporates completely, add a little more water. The chicken is done when the juices run clear when the thigh is pierced with a skewer. Transfer the chicken to a carving board and rest for 5 minutes, covered with tinfoil. Return the potatoes to the oven while the chicken is resting.

Carve the chicken into pieces and arrange on a large heatproof serving dish with the potatoes around it and drizzle over any remaining juices. Sprinkle with the remaining herbs and serve.

Try This: FOR AN ALTERNATIVE: 226   FOR PUDDING: 296

Chicken with Roasted Fennel & Citrus Rice

SERVES 4

2 tsp fennel seeds
1 tbsp freshly
    chopped oregano
1 garlic clove, peeled
    and crushed
salt and freshly ground
    black pepper
4 chicken quarters,
    about 175 g/6 oz each

½ lemon, finely sliced
1 fennel bulb, trimmed
2 tsp olive oil
4 plum tomatoes
25 g/1 oz stoned green olives

For the citrus rice
225 g/8 oz long-grain rice
finely grated rind and juice

of ½ lemon
150 ml/¼ pint orange juice
450 ml/¾ pint boiling chicken
    or vegetable stock

To garnish:
fennel fronds
orange slices

Preheat the oven to 200°C/400°F/Gas Mark 6. Lightly crush the fennel seeds and mix with oregano, garlic, salt and pepper. Place between the skin and flesh of the chicken breasts, careful not to tear the skin. Arrange the lemon slices on top of the chicken.

Cut the fennel into 8 wedges. Place on a baking tray with the chicken. Lightly brush the fennel with the oil. Cook the chicken and fennel on the top shelf of the preheated oven for 10 minutes.

Meanwhile, put the rice in a 2.3 litre/4 pint ovenproof dish. Stir in the lemon rind and juice, orange juice and stock. Cover with a lid and put on the middle shelf of the oven.

Reduce the oven temperature to 180°C/350°F/Gas Mark 4. Cook the chicken for a further 40 minutes, turning the fennel wedges and lemon slices once. Deseed and chop the tomatoes. Add to the tray and cook for 5–10 minutes. Remove from the oven.

When cooled slightly, remove the chicken skin and discard. Fluff the rice, scatter olives over the dish. Garnish with fennel fronds, orange slices and serve.

Try This: FOR AN ALTERNATIVE: 250   FOR PUDDING: 308

Braised Chicken in Beer

SERVES 4

4 chicken joints, skinned
125 g/4 oz pitted dried
   prunes
2 bay leaves
12 shallots
2 tsp olive oil
125 g/4 oz small button
   mushrooms, wiped

1 tsp soft dark brown sugar
½ tsp whole-grain mustard
2 tsp tomato purée
150 ml/¼ pint light ale
150 ml/¼ pint chicken stock
salt and freshly ground
   black pepper
2 tsp cornflour

2 tsp lemon juice
2 tbsp chopped fresh parsley
flat-leaf parsley, to garnish

To serve:
mashed potatoes
seasonal green vegetables

Preheat the oven to 170°C/325°F/Gas Mark 3. Cut each chicken joint in half and put in an ovenproof casserole with the prunes and bay leaves.

To peel the shallots, put in a small bowl and cover with boiling water. Drain after 2 minutes and rinse under cold water until cool enough to handle. The skins should then peel away easily from the shallots. Heat the oil in a large non-stick frying pan. Add the shallots and gently cook for about 5 minutes until beginning to colour. Add the mushrooms to the pan and cook for a further 3–4 minutes until both the mushrooms and onions are softened. Sprinkle the sugar over the shallots and mushrooms, then add the mustard, tomato purée, ale and chicken stock. Season to taste with salt and pepper and bring to the boil, stirring to combine. Carefully pour over the chicken. Cover the casserole and cook in the preheated oven for 1 hour.

Blend the cornflour with the lemon juice and 1 tablespoon of cold water and stir into the chicken casserole. Return the casserole to the oven for a further 10 minutes or until the chicken is cooked and the vegetables are tender.

Remove the bay leaves and stir in the chopped parsley. Garnish the chicken with the flat-leaf parsley. Serve with the mashed potatoes and fresh green vegetables.

Try This: FOR AN ALTERNATIVE: 240   FOR PUDDING: 314

Chilli Roast Chicken

SERVES 4

3 medium-hot fresh red
  chillies, deseeded
½ tsp ground turmeric
1 tsp cumin seeds
1 tsp coriander seeds
2 garlic cloves, peeled
  and crushed
2.5 cm/1 inch piece fresh
  root ginger, peeled

  and chopped
1 tbsp lemon juice
1 tbsp olive oil
2 tbsp roughly chopped
  fresh coriander
½ tsp salt
freshly ground black pepper
1.4 kg/3 lb oven-ready
  chicken

15 g/½ oz unsalted
  butter, melted
550 g/1¼ lb butternut squash
fresh parsley and coriander
  sprigs, to garnish

To serve:
4 baked potatoes
seasonal green vegetables

Preheat the oven to 190°C/375°F/Gas Mark 5. Roughly chop the chillies and put in a food processor with the turmeric, cumin seeds, coriander seeds, garlic, ginger, lemon juice, olive oil, coriander, salt, pepper and 2 tablespoons of cold water. Blend to a paste, leaving the ingredients still slightly chunky.

Starting at the neck end of the chicken, gently ease up the skin to loosen it from the breast. Reserve 3 tablespoons of the paste. Push the remaining paste over the chicken breast under the skin, spreading it evenly.

Put the chicken in a large roasting tin. Mix the reserved chilli paste with the melted butter. Use 1 tablespoon to brush evenly over the chicken, roast in the preheated oven for 20 minutes.

Meanwhile, halve, peel and scoop out the seeds from the butternut squash. Cut into large chunks and mix in the remaining chilli paste and butter mixture. Arrange the butternut squash around the chicken. Roast for a further hour, basting with the cooking juices about every 20 minutes until the chicken is fully cooked and the squash tender. Garnish with parsley and coriander. Serve hot with baked potatoes and green vegetables.

Try This: FOR AN ALTERNATIVE: 232   FOR PUDDING: 336

Herbed Hasselback Potatoes with Roast Chicken

SERVES 4

8 medium, evenly-sized potatoes, peeled
3 large sprigs of fresh rosemary
1 tbsp oil
salt and freshly ground black pepper
350 g/12 oz baby parsnips, peeled
350 g/12 oz baby carrots, peeled
350 g/12 oz baby leeks, trimmed
75 g/3 oz butter
finely grated rind of 1 lemon, preferably unwaxed
1.6 kg/3½ lb chicken

Preheat the oven to 200°C/400°F/Gas Mark 6, about 15 minutes before cooking. Place a chopstick on either side of a potato and, with a sharp knife, cut down through the potato until you reach the chopsticks; take care not to cut right through the potato. Repeat these cuts every 5 mm/¼ inch along the length of the potato. Carefully ease 2–4 of the slices apart and slip in a few rosemary sprigs. Repeat with remaining potatoes. Brush with the oil and season well with salt and pepper.

Place the seasoned potatoes in a large roasting tin. Add the parsnips, carrots and leeks to the potatoes in the tin, cover with a wire rack or trivet.

Beat the butter and lemon rind together and season to taste. Smear the chicken with the lemon butter and place on the rack over the vegetables.

Roast in the preheated oven for 1 hour 40 minutes, basting the chicken and vegetables occasionally, until cooked thoroughly. The juices should run clear when the thigh is pierced with a skewer. Place the cooked chicken on a warmed serving platter, arrange the roast vegetables around it and serve immediately.

Try This: FOR AN ALTERNATIVE: 218   FOR PUDDING: 298

Cheesy Chicken Burgers

SERVES 4

1 tbsp sunflower oil
1 small onion, peeled and
　finely chopped
1 garlic clove, peeled
　and crushed
½ red pepper, deseeded and
　finely chopped
450 g/1 lb fresh chicken mince
2 tbsp 0%-fat Greek yogurt
50 g/2 oz fresh
　brown breadcrumbs

1 tbsp freshly chopped
　herbs, such as parsley or
　tarragon
50 g/2 oz Cheshire
　cheese, crumbled
salt and freshly ground
　black pepper

**For the sweetcorn and
　tomato relish:**
200 g can sweetcorn, drained

1 carrot, peeled, grated
½ green chilli, deseeded
　and finely chopped
2 tsp cider vinegar
2 tsp light soft brown sugar

To serve:
wholemeal or granary rolls
lettuce
sliced tomatoes
mixed salad leaves

Preheat the grill. Heat the oil in a frying pan and gently cook the onion and garlic for 5 minutes. Add the red pepper and cook for 5 minutes. Transfer into a mixing bowl and reserve.

Add the chicken, yogurt, breadcrumbs, herbs and cheese and season to taste with salt and pepper. Mix well. Divide the mixture equally into 6 and shape into burgers. Cover and chill in the refrigerator for at least 20 minutes.

To make the relish, put all the ingredients in a small saucepan with 1 tablespoon of water and heat gently, stirring occasionally until all the sugar has dissolved. Cover and cook over a low heat for 2 minutes, then uncover and cook for a further minute, or until the relish is thick.

Place the burgers on a lightly oiled grill pan and grill under a medium heat for 8–10 minutes on each side, or until browned and completely cooked through.

Warm the rolls if liked, then split in half and fill with the burgers, lettuce, sliced tomatoes and the prepared relish. Serve immediately with the salad leaves.

Try This: FOR AN ALTERNATIVE: 264　FOR PUDDING: 374

Chicken & Summer Vegetable Risotto

SERVES 4

1 litre/1¾ pint chicken or vegetable stock
225 g/8 oz baby asparagus spears
125 g/4 oz French beans
15 g/½ oz butter
1 small onion, peeled and finely chopped
150 ml/¼ pint dry white wine
275 g/10 oz arborio rice
pinch of saffron strands
75 g/3 oz frozen peas, thawed
225 g/8 oz cooked chicken, skinned and diced
juice of ½ lemon
salt and freshly ground black pepper
25 g/1 oz Parmesan, shaved

Bring the stock to the boil in a large saucepan. Trim the asparagus and cut into 4 cm/1½ inch lengths. Blanch the asparagus in the stock for 1–2 minutes or until tender, then remove with a slotted spoon and reserve. Halve the green beans and cook in the boiling stock for 4 minutes. Remove and reserve. Turn down the heat and keep the stock barely simmering.

Melt the butter in a heavy-based saucepan. Add the onion and cook gently for about 5 minutes. Pour the wine into the pan and boil rapidly until the liquid has almost reduced. Add the rice and cook, stirring for 1 minute until the grains are coated and look translucent.

Add the saffron and a ladle of the stock. Simmer, stirring all the time, until the stock has absorbed. Continue adding the stock, a ladle at a time, until it has all been absorbed. After 15 minutes the risotto should be creamy with a slight bite to it. If not add a little more stock and cook for a few more minutes, or until it is of the correct texture and consistency. Add the peas, reserved vegetables, chicken and lemon juice. Season to taste with salt and pepper and cook for 3-4 minutes or until the chicken is thoroughly heated and piping hot.

Spoon the risotto on to warmed serving plates. Scatter each portion with a few shavings of Parmesan cheese and serve immediately.

Try This: FOR AN ALTERNATIVE: 236   FOR PUDDING: 316

Mexican Chicken

SERVES 4

1.4 kg/3 lb oven-ready
  chicken, jointed
3 tbsp plain flour
½ tsp ground paprika pepper
salt and freshly ground
  black pepper
2 tsp sunflower oil
1 small onion, peeled
  and chopped
1 red chilli, deseeded and

finely chopped
½ tsp ground cumin
½ tsp dried oregano
300 ml/½ pint chicken or
  vegetable stock
1 green pepper, deseeded
  and sliced
2 tsp cocoa powder
1 tbsp lime juice
2 tsp clear honey

3 tbsp 0%-fat Greek yogurt

To garnish:
sliced limes
red chilli slices
sprig of fresh oregano

To serve:
freshly cooked rice
fresh green salad leaves

Using a knife, remove the skin from the chicken joints. In a shallow dish, mix together the flour, paprika, salt and pepper. Coat the chicken on both sides with flour and shake off any excess if necessary. Heat the oil in a large non-stick frying pan. Add the chicken and brown on both sides. Transfer to a plate and reserve.

Add the onion and red chilli to the pan and gently cook for 5 minutes, or until the onion is soft. Stir occasionally. Stir in the cumin and oregano and cook for a further minute. Pour in the stock and bring to the boil. Return the chicken to the pan, cover and cook for 40 minutes. Add the green pepper and cook for 10 minutes, until the chicken is cooked. Remove the chicken and pepper with a slotted spoon and keep warm in a serving dish.

Blend the cocoa powder with 1 tablespoon of warm water. Stir into the sauce, then boil rapidly until the sauce has thickened and reduced by about one third. Stir in the lime juice, honey and yogurt. Pour the sauce over the chicken and pepper and garnish with the lime slices, chilli and oregano. Serve immediately with the freshly cooked rice and green salad.

Try This: FOR AN ALTERNATIVE: 224   FOR PUDDING: 360

Chicken Basquaise

SERVES 4–6

1.4 kg/3 lb chicken, cut into 8 pieces
2 tbsp plain flour
salt and freshly ground black pepper
3 tbsp olive oil
1 large onion, peeled and sliced
2 red peppers, deseeded and cut into thick strips
2 garlic cloves, peeled and crushed
150 g/5 oz spicy chorizo sausage cut into 1 cm/½ inch pieces
200 g/7 oz long-grain white rice
450 ml/¾ pint chicken stock
1 tsp crushed dried chillies
½ tsp dried thyme
1 tbsp tomato purée
125 g/4 oz Spanish air-dried ham, diced
12 black olives
2 tbsp freshly chopped parsley

Dry the chicken pieces well with absorbent kitchen paper. Put the flour in a polythene bag, season with salt and pepper and add the chicken pieces. Twist the bag to seal, then shake to coat the chicken pieces thoroughly. Heat 2 tablespoons of the oil in a large heavy-based saucepan over a medium-high heat. Add the chicken pieces and cook for about 15 minutes, turning on all sides, until well browned. Using a slotted spoon, transfer to a plate.

Add the remaining olive oil to the saucepan, then add the onion and peppers. Reduce the heat to medium and cook, stirring frequently, until starting to colour and soften. Stir in the garlic and chorizo and continue to cook for a further 3 minutes. Add the rice and cook for about 2 minutes, stirring to coat with the oil, until the rice is translucent and golden. Stir in the stock, crushed chillies, thyme, tomato purée and salt and pepper and bring to the boil. Return the chicken to the saucepan, pressing gently into the rice. Cover and cook over a very low heat for about 45 minutes until the chicken and rice are cooked and tender.

Gently stir in the ham, black olives and half the parsley. Cover and heat for a further 5 minutes. Sprinkle with the remaining parsley and serve immediately.

Try This: FOR AN ALTERNATIVE: 236 FOR PUDDING: 380

Chicken & Seafood Risotto

SERVES 6–8

125 ml/4 fl oz olive oil
1.4 kg/3 lb chicken, cut into 8 pieces
350 g/12 oz spicy chorizo sausage, cut into 1 cm/½ inch pieces
125 g/4 oz cured ham, diced
1 onion, peeled and chopped
2 red or yellow peppers, deseeded and cut into 2.5 cm/1 inch pieces

4 garlic cloves, peeled and finely chopped
750 g/1 lb 10 oz short-grain Spanish rice or Arborio rice
2 bay leaves
1 tsp dried thyme
1 tsp saffron strands, lightly crushed
200 ml/7 fl oz dry white wine
1.6 l/2¾ pt chicken stock

salt and freshly ground black pepper
125 g/4 oz fresh shelled peas
450 g/1 lb uncooked prawns
36 clams and/or mussels, well scrubbed
2 tbsp freshly chopped parsley

To garnish:
lemon wedges
fresh parsley sprigs

Heat half the oil in a 45.5 cm/18 inch paella pan or deep wide frying pan. Add the chicken pieces and fry for 15 minutes, turning constantly, until golden. Remove from the pan and reserve. Add the chorizo and ham to the pan and cook for 6 minutes until crisp, stirring occasionally. Remove and add to the chicken. Add the onion to the pan and cook for 3 minutes, or until beginning to soften. Add the peppers and garlic and cook for 2 minutes; add to the reserved chicken, chorizo and ham.

Add the remaining oil to the pan and stir in the rice until well coated. Stir in the bay leaves, thyme and saffron, then pour in the wine and bubble until evaporated, stirring and scraping up any bits on the bottom of the pan. Stir in the stock and bring to the boil, stirring occasionally.

Return the chicken, chorizo, ham and vegetables to the pan, burying them gently in the rice. Season to taste with salt and pepper. Reduce the heat and simmer for 10 minutes, stirring occasionally. Add the peas and seafood, pushing them gently into the rice. Cover, cook over a low heat for 5 minutes, or until the rice and prawns are tender and the clams and mussels open (discard any that do not open). Stand for 5 minutes. Sprinkle with the parsley, garnish and serve.

Try This: FOR AN ALTERNATIVE: 230   FOR PUDDING: 366

Creamy Chicken & Rice Pilau

SERVES 6–8

350 g/12 oz basmati rice
salt and freshly ground black
    pepper
50 g/2 oz butter
100 g/3½ oz flaked almonds
75 g/3 oz unsalted shelled
    pistachio nuts
4–6 skinless chicken breast
    fillets, each cut into 4
    pieces

2 tbsp vegetable oil
2 medium onions, peeled
    and thinly sliced
2 garlic cloves, peeled and
    finely chopped
2.5 cm/1 inch piece of fresh
    root ginger, finely chopped
6 green cardamom pods,
    lightly crushed
4–6 whole cloves

1 tsp ground coriander
½ tsp cayenne pepper, or to
    taste
2 bay leaves
225 ml/8 fl oz natural yogurt
225 ml/8 fl oz double cream
225 g/8 oz seedless green
    grapes, halved if large
2 tbsp freshly chopped
    coriander or mint

Bring a saucepan of lightly salted water to the boil. Gradually pour in the rice; return to the boil, then simmer for about 12 minutes until tender. Drain, rinse under cold water and reserve.

Heat the butter in a large deep frying pan over a medium-high heat. Add the almonds and pistachios and cook for about 2 minutes, stirring constantly, until golden. Using a slotted spoon, transfer to a plate.

Add the chicken pieces to the pan and cook for 5 minutes, or until golden, turning once. Remove from the pan and reserve. Add the oil to the pan and cook the onions for 10 minutes, or until golden, stirring frequently. Stir in the garlic, ginger, spices and bay leaves and cook for 2–3 minutes, stirring. Add 2–3 tablespoons of the yogurt and cook, stirring until the moisture evaporates. Continue adding the yogurt in this way until it is used up.

Return the chicken and nuts to the pan and stir. Stir in 125 ml/4 fl oz of boiling water and season to taste with salt and pepper. Cook, covered, over a low heat for 10 minutes until the chicken is tender. Stir in the cream, grapes and half the herbs. Gently fold in the rice. Heat through for 5 minutes and sprinkle with the remaining herbs, then serve.

Try This: FOR AN ALTERNATIVE: 242 FOR PUDDING: 308

Creamy Chicken Stroganoff

SERVES 4

450 g/1 lb skinless chicken breast fillets
4 tbsp dry sherry
15 g/½ oz dried porcini mushrooms
2 tbsp sunflower oil
25 g/1 oz unsalted butter
1 onion, peeled and sliced

225 g/8 oz chestnut mushrooms, wiped and sliced
1 tbsp paprika
1 tsp freshly chopped thyme
125 ml/4 fl oz chicken stock
150 ml/¼ pint crème fraîche
salt and freshly ground

black pepper
sprigs of fresh thyme, to garnish

To serve:
crème fraîche
freshly cooked rice or egg noodles

Cut the chicken into finger-length strips and reserve. Gently warm the sherry in a small saucepan and remove from the heat. Add the porcini mushrooms and leave to soak while preparing the rest of the stir-fry.

Heat a wok, add 1½ tablespoons of the oil and when hot, add the chicken and stir-fry over a high heat for 3–4 minutes, or until lightly browned. Remove from the wok and reserve.

Heat the remaining oil and butter in the wok and gently cook the onion for 5 minutes. Add the chestnut mushrooms and stir-fry for a further 5 minutes, or until tender. Sprinkle in the paprika and thyme and cook for 30 seconds.

Add the porcini mushrooms with their soaking liquid, then stir in the stock and return the chicken to the wok. Cook for 1–2 minutes, or until the chicken is cooked through and tender.

Stir in the crème fraîche and heat until piping hot. Season to taste with salt and pepper. Garnish with sprigs of fresh thyme and serve immediately with a spoonful of crème fraîche and rice or egg noodles.

Try This: FOR AN ALTERNATIVE: 222   FOR PUDDING: 330

Chicken & White Wine Risotto

SERVES 4–6

2 tbsp oil
125 g/4 oz unsalted butter
2 shallots, peeled and finely
    chopped
300 g/11 oz Arborio rice
600 ml/1 pint dry white wine

750 ml/1¼ pints chicken
    stock, heated
350 g/12 oz skinless chicken
    breast fillets, thinly sliced
50 g/2 oz Parmesan cheese,
    grated

2 tbsp freshly chopped dill
    or parsley
salt and freshly ground black
    pepper

Heat the oil and half the butter in a large heavy-based saucepan over a medium-high heat. Add the shallots and cook for 2 minutes, or until softened, stirring frequently. Add the rice and cook for 2–3 minutes, stirring frequently, until the rice is translucent and well coated.

Pour in half the wine; it will bubble and steam rapidly. Cook, stirring constantly, until the liquid is absorbed. Add a ladleful of the hot stock and cook until the liquid is absorbed. Carefully stir in the chicken.

Continue adding the stock, about half a ladleful at a time, allowing each addition to be absorbed before adding the next; never allow the rice to cook dry. This process should take about 20 minutes. The risotto should have a creamy consistency and the rice should be tender, but firm to the bite.

Stir in the remaining wine and cook for 2–3 minutes. Remove from the heat and stir in the remaining butter with the Parmesan cheese and half the chopped herbs. Season to taste with salt and pepper. Spoon into warmed shallow bowls and sprinkle each with the remaining chopped herbs. Serve immediately.

Try This: FOR AN ALTERNATIVE: 238   FOR PUDDING: 356

Chicken Pie with Sweet Potato Topping

SERVES 4

250 g/9 oz potatoes, peeled and cut into chunks
700 g/1½ lb sweet potatoes, peeled and cut into chunks
150 ml/¼ pint milk
25 g/1 oz butter
2 tsp brown sugar
grated rind of 1 orange

salt and freshly ground black pepper
4 skinless chicken breast fillets, diced
1 medium onion, peeled and coarsely chopped
125 g/4 oz baby mushrooms, stems trimmed
2 leeks, trimmed and

thickly sliced
150 ml/¼ pint dry white wine
1 chicken stock cube
1 tbsp freshly chopped parsley
50 ml/2 fl oz crème fraîche or thick double cream
green vegetables, to serve

Preheat the oven to 190°C/375°F/Gas Mark 5, 10 minutes before required. Cook the potatoes and sweet potatoes in lightly salted boiling water until tender. Drain well, then return to the saucepan and mash until smooth and creamy, gradually adding the milk, then the butter, sugar and orange rind. Season to taste with salt and pepper and reserve.

Place the chicken in a saucepan with the onion, mushrooms, leeks, wine, stock cube and season to taste. Simmer, covered, until the chicken and vegetables are tender. Using a slotted spoon, transfer the chicken and vegetables to a 1.1 litre/2 pint pie dish. Add the parsley and crème fraîche or cream to the liquid in the pan and bring to the boil. Simmer until thickened and smooth, stirring constantly. Pour over the chicken in the pie dish, mix and cool.

Spread the mashed potato over the chicken filling, and swirl the surface into decorative peaks. Bake in the preheated oven for 35 minutes, or until the top is golden and the chicken filling is heated through. Serve immediately with fresh green vegetables.

Try This: FOR AN ALTERNATIVE: 240   FOR PUDDING: 340

Chinese–style Fried Rice

SERVES 4–6

2–3 tbsp groundnut oil or vegetable oil
2 small onions, peeled and cut into wedges
2 garlic cloves, peeled and thinly sliced
2.5 cm/1 inch piece of fresh root ginger, peeled and cut into thin slivers
225 g/8 oz cooked chicken, thinly sliced
125 g/4 oz cooked ham, thinly sliced
350 g/12 oz cooked cold long-grain white rice
125 g/4 oz canned water chestnuts, sliced
225 g/8 oz cooked peeled prawns (optional)
3 large eggs
3 tsp sesame oil
salt and freshly ground black pepper
6 spring onions, trimmed and sliced into 1 cm/ ½ inch pieces
2 tbsp dark soy sauce
1 tbsp sweet chilli sauce
2 tbsp freshly chopped coriander

To garnish:
2 tbsp chopped roasted peanuts
sprig of fresh coriander

Heat a wok or large deep frying pan until very hot, add the oil and heat for 30 seconds. Add the onions and stir-fry for 2 minutes. Stir in the garlic and ginger and cook for 1 minute. Add the cooked sliced chicken and ham and stir-fry for a further 2–3 minutes.

Add the rice, the water chestnuts and prawns, if using, with 2 tablespoons of water, and stir-fry for 2 minutes until the rice is heated through.

Beat the eggs with 1 teaspoon of the sesame oil and season to taste with salt and pepper. Make a well in the centre of the rice, then pour in the egg mixture and stir immediately, gradually drawing the rice mixture into the egg, until the egg is cooked.

Add the spring onions, soy and chilli sauces, coriander and a little water, if necessary. Adjust the seasoning and drizzle with the remaining sesame oil. Sprinkle with the nuts, garnish and serve.

 Try This: FOR AN ALTERNATIVE: 238   FOR PUDDING: 314

Sticky–glazed Spatchcocked Poussins

SERVES 4

2 poussins, each about
700 g/1½ lb
salt and freshly ground
black pepper
4 kumquats, thinly sliced
assorted salad leaves,
crusty bread or new

potatoes, to serve

For the glaze:
zest of 1 small lemon,
finely grated
1 tbsp lemon juice
1 tbsp dry sherry

2 tbsp clear honey
2 tbsp dark soy sauce
2 tbsp whole-grain mustard
1 tsp tomato purée
½ tsp Chinese five-
spice powder

Preheat the grill just before cooking. Place one of the poussins breast-side down on a board. Using poultry shears, cut down one side of the backbone. Cut down the other side of the backbone. Remove the bone. Open out the poussin and press down hard on the breast bone with the heel of your hand to break it and to flatten the poussin.

Thread two skewers crosswise through the bird to keep it flat, ensuring that each skewer goes through a wing and out through the leg on the opposite side. Repeat with the other bird. Season both sides of the bird with salt and pepper.

To make the glaze, mix together the lemon zest and juice, sherry, honey, soy sauce, mustard, tomato purée and Chinese five-spice powder and use to brush all over the poussins.

Place the poussins skin-side down on a grill rack and grill under a medium heat for 15 minutes, brushing halfway through with more glaze. Turn the poussins over and grill for 10 minutes. Brush again with glaze and arrange the kumquat slices on top. Grill for a further 15 minutes until well-browned and cooked through. If they start to brown too quickly, turn down the grill a little.

Remove the skewers and cut each poussin in half along the breastbone. Serve immediately with the salad, crusty bread or new potatoes.

Fruity Rice–stuffed Poussins

SERVES 6

For the rice stuffing:
225 ml/8 fl oz port
125 g/4 oz raisins
125 g/4 oz ready-to-eat dried
    apricots, chopped
2 tbsp olive oil
1 medium onion, peeled and
    finely chopped
1 celery stalk, trimmed and
    finely sliced
2 garlic cloves, peeled and
    finely chopped

1½ tsp mixed spice
1 tsp each dried oregano
    and mint or basil
225 g/8 oz unsweetened
    canned chestnuts,
    chopped
200 g/7 oz long-grain white
    rice, cooked
grated rind and juice of 2
    oranges
350 ml/12 fl oz chicken stock
50 g/2 oz walnut halves,

lightly toasted and chopped
2 tbsp each freshly chopped
    mint and parsley
salt and freshly ground black
    pepper

6 oven-ready poussins
50 g/2 oz butter, melted

To garnish:
fresh herbs
orange wedges

Preheat the oven to 180°C/350°F/Gas Mark 4. To make the stuffing, place the port, raisins and apricots in a bowl and leave for 15 minutes. Heat the oil in a large saucepan. Add the onion and celery and cook for 3–4 minutes. Add the garlic, mixed spice, herbs and chestnuts and cook for 4 minutes, stirring occasionally. Add the rice, half the orange rind and juice and the stock. Simmer for 5 minutes until most liquid is absorbed. Drain the raisins and apricots, reserving the port. Stir into the rice with the walnuts, mint, parsley and seasoning and cook for 2 minutes. Remove and cool.

Rinse the poussin cavities, pat dry and season with salt and pepper. Lightly fill the cavities with the stuffing. Tie the legs together, tucking in the tail. Form any extra stuffing into balls.

Place in roasting tins with stuffing balls and brush with melted butter. Drizzle over the remaining butter, remaining orange rind and juice and port. Roast in the preheated oven for 50 minutes or until golden and cooked, basting every 15 minutes. Transfer to a platter, cover with tinfoil and rest. Pour over any pan juices. Garnish with herbs and orange wedges. Serve with the stuffing.

Try This: FOR AN ALTERNATIVE: 220   FOR PUDDING: 376

Potato–stuffed Roast Poussin

SERVES 4

4 oven-ready poussins
salt and freshly ground black
    pepper
1 lemon, cut into quarters
450 g/1 lb floury potatoes,
    peeled and cut into 4 cm/
    1½ inch pieces

1 tbsp freshly chopped
    thyme or rosemary
3–4 tbsp olive oil
4 garlic cloves, unpeeled
    and lightly smashed
8 slices streaky bacon or
    Parma ham

125 ml/4 fl oz white wine
2 spring onions, trimmed
    and thinly sliced
2 tbsp double cream or
    crème fraîche
lemon wedges, to garnish

Preheat the oven to 220°C/425°F/Gas Mark 7. Place a roasting tin in the oven to heat. Rinse the poussin cavities and pat dry with absorbent kitchen paper. Season the cavities with salt and pepper and a squeeze of lemon. Push a lemon quarter into each cavity.

Put the potatoes in a saucepan of lightly salted water and bring to the boil. Reduce the heat to low and simmer until just tender; do not overcook. Drain and cool slightly. Sprinkle the chopped herbs over the potatoes and drizzle with 2–3 tablespoons of the oil.

Spoon half the potatoes into the poussin cavities – not too tightly. Rub each poussin with a little oil and season with pepper. Carefully spoon 1 tablespoon of oil into the hot roasting tin and arrange the poussins with the remaining potatoes around the edge. Sprinkle over the garlic.

Roast the poussins in the preheated oven for 30 minutes, or until the skin is golden and beginning to crisp. Carefully lay the bacon slices over the breast of each poussin and continue to roast for 15–20 minutes until crisp and the poussins are cooked through. Transfer the poussins and potatoes to a serving platter and cover loosely with tinfoil. Skim off the fat from the juices. Place the tin over a medium heat, add the wine and spring onions. Cook briefly, scraping the bits from the bottom of the tin. Whisk in the cream or crème fraîche and bubble for 1 minute, or until thickened. Garnish the poussins with lemon wedges, and serve with the creamy gravy.

Try This: FOR AN ALTERNATIVE: 250   FOR PUDDING: 324

Turkey Hash with Potato & Beetroot

SERVES 4–6

2 tbsp vegetable oil
50 g/2 oz butter
4 slices streaky bacon, diced or sliced
1 medium onion, peeled and finely chopped

450 g/1 lb cooked turkey, diced
450 g/1 lb finely chopped cooked potatoes
2–3 tbsp freshly chopped parsley

2 tbsp plain flour
250 g/9 oz cooked medium beetroot, diced
green salad, to serve

In a large, heavy-based frying pan, heat the oil and half the butter over a medium heat until sizzling. Add the bacon and cook for 4 minutes, or until crisp and golden, stirring occasionally. Using a slotted spoon, transfer to a large bowl. Add the onion to the pan and cook for 3–4 minutes, or until soft and golden, stirring frequently.

Meanwhile, add the turkey, potatoes, parsley and flour to the cooked bacon in the bowl. Stir and toss gently, then fold in the diced beetroot.

Add half the remaining butter to the frying pan and then the turkey vegetable mixture. Stir, then spread the mixture to evenly cover the bottom of the frying pan. Cook for 15 minutes, or until the underside is crisp and brown, pressing the hash firmly into a cake with a spatula. Remove from the heat.

Invert a large plate over the frying pan and, holding the plate and frying pan together with an oven glove, turn the hash out onto the plate. Heat the remaining butter in the pan, slide the hash back into the pan and cook for 4 minutes, or until crisp and brown on the other side. Invert onto the plate again and serve immediately with a green salad.

  Try This: FOR AN ALTERNATIVE: 234 FOR PUDDING: 306

Turkey & Tomato Tagine

SERVES 4

For the meatballs:
450 g/1 lb fresh turkey mince
1 small onion, peeled and
   very finely chopped
1 garlic clove, peeled
   and crushed
1 tbsp freshly
   chopped coriander
1 tsp ground cumin
1 tbsp olive oil

salt and freshly ground
   black pepper

For the sauce:
1 onion, peeled and
   finely chopped
1 garlic clove, peeled
   and crushed
150 ml/¼ pint turkey stock
400 g can chopped tomatoes

½ tsp ground cumin
½ tsp ground cinnamon
pinch of cayenne pepper
freshly chopped parsley
freshly chopped herbs,
   to garnish
freshly cooked couscous or
   rice, to serve

Preheat the oven to 190°C/375°F/Gas Mark 5. Put all the ingredients for the meatballs in a bowl, except the oil and mix well. Season to taste with salt and pepper. Shape into 20 balls, about the size of walnuts. Put on a tray, cover lightly and chill in the refrigerator while making the sauce.

Put the onion and garlic in a pan with 125 ml/4 fl oz of the stock. Cook over a low heat until all the stock has evaporated. Continue cooking for 1 minute, or until the onions begin to colour. Add the remaining stock to the pan with the tomatoes, cumin, cinnamon and cayenne pepper. Simmer for 10 minutes, until slightly thickened and reduced. Stir in the parsley and season to taste.

Heat the oil in a large non-stick frying pan and cook the meatballs in two batches until lightly browned all over. Lift the meatballs out with a slotted spoon and drain on kitchen paper.

Pour the sauce into a tagine or an ovenproof casserole. Top with the meatballs, cover and cook in the preheated oven for 25–30 minutes, or until the meatballs are cooked through and the sauce is bubbling. Garnish with freshly chopped herbs and serve immediately on a bed of couscous or plain boiled rice.

Try This: FOR AN ALTERNATIVE: 208   FOR PUDDING: 358

Pies & Puddings: Poultry

Turkey & Pesto Rice Roulades

SERVES 4

125 g/4 oz cooked white rice,
    at room temperature
1 garlic clove, peeled and
    crushed
1–2 tbsp Parmesan cheese,
    grated
2 tbsp prepared pesto sauce
2 tbsp pine nuts, lightly

    toasted and chopped
4 turkey steaks, each
    weighing about 150 g/5 oz
salt and freshly ground black
    pepper
4 slices Parma ham
2 tbsp olive oil
50 ml/2 fl oz white wine

25 g/1 oz unsalted butter,
    chilled

To serve:
freshly cooked spinach
freshly cooked pasta

Put the rice in a bowl and add the garlic, Parmesan cheese, pesto and pine nuts. Stir to combine the ingredients, then reserve.

Place the turkey steaks on a chopping board and, using a sharp knife, cut horizontally through each steak, without cutting right through. Open up the steaks and cover with baking parchment. Flatten slightly by pounding with a meat mallet or rolling pin.

Season each steak with salt and pepper. Divide the stuffing equally among the steaks, spreading evenly over one half. Fold the steaks in half to enclose the filling, then wrap each steak in a slice of Parma ham and secure with cocktail sticks.

Heat the oil in a large frying pan over medium heat. Cook the steaks for 5 minutes, or until golden on one side. Turn and cook for a further 2 minutes. Push the steaks to the side and pour in the wine. Allow the wine to bubble and evaporate. Add the butter, a little at a time, whisking constantly until the sauce is smooth. Discard the cocktail sticks, then serve the steaks drizzled with the sauce and serve with spinach and pasta.

Try This: FOR AN ALTERNATIVE: 252 FOR PUDDING: 364

Guinea Fowl with Calvados & Apples

SERVES 4

4 guinea fowl supremes,
   each about 150 g/5 oz,
   skinned
1 tbsp plain flour
1 tbsp sunflower oil
1 onion, peeled and
   finely sliced
1 garlic clove, peeled

and crushed
1 tsp freshly chopped thyme
150 ml/¼ pint dry cider
salt and freshly ground
   black pepper
3 tbsp Calvados brandy
sprigs of fresh thyme,
   to garnish

For the caramelised apples:
15 g/½ oz unsalted butter
2 red-skinned eating apples,
   quartered, cored and
   sliced
1 tsp caster sugar

Lightly dust the guinea fowl supremes with the flour. Heat 2 teaspoons of the oil in a large non-stick frying pan and cook the supremes for 2–3 minutes on each side until browned. Remove from the pan and reserve.

Heat the remaining teaspoon of oil in the pan and add the onion and garlic. Cook over a medium heat for 10 minutes, stirring occasionally until soft and just beginning to colour. Stir in the chopped thyme and cider. Return the guinea fowl to the pan, season with salt and pepper and bring to a very gentle simmer. Cover and cook over a low heat for 15–20 minutes or until the guinea fowl is tender. Remove the guinea fowl and keep warm. Turn up the heat and boil the sauce until thickened and reduced by half.

Meanwhile, prepare the apples. Melt the butter in a small non-stick pan, add the apple slices in a single layer and sprinkle with the sugar. Cook until the apples are tender and beginning to caramelise, turning once. Put the Calvados in a metal ladle or small saucepan and gently heat until warm. Carefully set alight with a match, let the flames die down, then stir into the sauce.

Serve the guinea fowl with the sauce spooned over and garnished with the caramelised apples and sprigs of fresh thyme.

Try This: FOR AN ALTERNATIVE: 222   FOR PUDDING: 302

Duck with Berry Sauce

SERVES 4

4 x 175 g/6 oz boneless
  duck breasts
salt and freshly ground
  black pepper
1 tsp sunflower oil

For the sauce:
juice of 1 orange

1 bay leaf
3 tbsp redcurrant jelly
150 g/5 oz fresh or frozen
  mixed berries
2 tbsp dried cranberries
  or cherries
½ tsp soft light brown sugar
1 tbsp balsamic vinegar

1 tsp freshly chopped mint
sprigs of fresh mint, to
  garnish

To serve:
freshly cooked potatoes
freshly cooked green beans

Remove the skins from the duck breasts and season with a little salt and pepper. Brush a griddle pan with the oil, then heat on the stove until smoking hot.

Place the duck, skinned-side down in the pan. Cook over a medium-high heat for 5 minutes, or until well browned. Turn the duck and cook for 2 minutes. Lower the heat and cook for a further 5–8 minutes, or until cooked, but still slightly pink in the centre. Remove from the pan and keep warm.

While the duck is cooking, make the sauce. Put the orange juice, bay leaf, redcurrant jelly, fresh or frozen and dried berries and sugar in a small griddle pan. Add any juices left in the griddle pan to the small pan. Slowly bring to the boil, lower the heat and simmer uncovered for 4–5 minutes, until the fruit is soft.

Remove the bay leaf. Stir in the vinegar and chopped mint and season to taste with salt and pepper.

Slice the duck breasts on the diagonal and arrange on serving plates. Spoon over the berry sauce and garnish with sprigs of fresh mint. Serve immediately with the potatoes and green beans.

Try This: FOR AN ALTERNATIVE: 260   FOR PUDDING: 380

Aromatic Duck Burgers on Potato Pancakes

SERVES 4

700 g/1½ lb boneless duck
   breasts
2 tbsp hoisin sauce
1 garlic clove, peeled and
   finely chopped
4 spring onions, trimmed
   and finely chopped

2 tbsp Japanese soy sauce
½ tsp five-spice powder
salt and freshly ground black
   pepper
freshly chopped coriander,
   to garnish
extra hoisin sauce, to serve

For the potato pancakes:
450 g/1 lb floury potatoes
1 small onion, peeled and
   grated
1 small egg, beaten
1 heaped tbsp plain flour

Peel off the thick layer of fat from the duck breasts and cut into small pieces. Put the fat in a small dry saucepan and set over a low heat for 10–15 minutes, or until the fat runs clear and the crackling goes crisp; reserve. Cut the duck meat into pieces and blend in a food processor until coarsely chopped. Spoon into a bowl and add the hoisin sauce, garlic, half the spring onions, soy sauce and five-spice powder. Season to taste with salt and pepper and shape into 4 burgers. Cover and chill in the refrigerator for 1 hour.

To make the pancakes, grate the potatoes into a large bowl, squeeze out the water with your hands, then put on a clean tea towel and twist the ends to squeeze out any remaining water. Return to the bowl, add the onion and egg and mix well. Add the flour, salt and pepper. Stir to blend.

Heat about 2 tablespoons of the clear duck fat in a large frying pan. Spoon the potato mixture into 2–4 pattie shapes and cook for 6 minutes, or until golden and crisp, turning once. Keep warm in the oven. Repeat with the remaining mixture, adding duck fat as needed.

Preheat the grill and line the grill rack with tinfoil. Brush the burgers with a little of the duck fat and grill for 6–8 minutes, or longer if wished, turning once. Arrange 1–2 potato pancakes on a plate and top with a burger. Spoon over a little hoisin sauce and garnish with the remaining spring onions and coriander.

Try This: FOR AN ALTERNATIVE: 228   FOR PUDDING: 316

Vegetarian

Baked Macaroni Cheese

SERVES 8

450 g/1 lb macaroni
75 g/3 oz butter
1 onion, peeled and finely
   chopped
40 g/1½ oz plain flour
1 litre/1¾ pints milk
1–2 dried bay leaves
½ tsp dried thyme

salt and freshly ground black
   pepper
cayenne pepper
freshly grated nutmeg
2 small leeks, trimmed,
   finely chopped, cooked
   and drained
1 tbsp Dijon mustard

400 g/14 oz mature Cheddar
   cheese, grated
2 tbsp dried breadcrumbs
2 tbsp freshly grated
   Parmesan cheese
basil sprig, to garnish

Preheat the oven to 190°C/375°F/Gas Mark 5, 10 minutes before cooking. Bring a large pan of lightly salted water to a rolling boil. Add the macaroni and cook according to the packet instructions, or until *al dente*. Drain thoroughly and reserve.

Meanwhile, melt 50 g/2 oz of the butter in a large, heavy-based saucepan, add the onion and cook, stirring frequently, for 5–7 minutes, or until softened. Sprinkle in the flour and cook, stirring constantly, for 2 minutes. Remove the pan from the heat, stir in the milk, return to the heat and cook, stirring, until a smooth sauce has formed. Add the bay leaf and thyme to the sauce and season to taste with salt, pepper, cayenne pepper and freshly grated nutmeg. Simmer for about 15 minutes, stirring frequently, until thickened and smooth.

Remove the sauce from the heat. Add the cooked leeks, mustard and Cheddar cheese and stir until the cheese has melted. Stir in the macaroni then tip into a lightly oiled baking dish.

Sprinkle the breadcrumbs and Parmesan cheese over the macaroni. Dot with the remaining butter, then bake in the preheated oven for 1 hour, or until golden. Garnish with a basil sprig and serve immediately.

Try This: FOR AN ALTERNATIVE: 272   FOR PUDDING: 298

Vegetarian Spaghetti Bolognese

SERVES 4

2 tbsp olive oil
1 onion, peeled and
    finely chopped
1 carrot, peeled and
    finely chopped
1 celery stick, trimmed and
    finely chopped

225 g/8 oz Quorn mince
150 ml/5 fl oz red wine
300 ml/½ pint vegetable
    stock
1 tsp mushroom ketchup
4 tbsp tomato purée
350 g/12 oz dried spaghetti

4 tbsp half-fat crème fraîche
salt and freshly ground
    black pepper
1 tbsp freshly chopped
    parsley

Heat the oil in a large saucepan and add the onion, carrot and celery. Cook gently for 10 minutes, adding a little water if necessary, until softened and starting to brown.

Add the Quorn mince and cook a further 2–3 minutes before adding the red wine. Increase the heat and simmer gently until nearly all the wine has evaporated.

Mix together the vegetable stock and mushroom ketchup and add about half to the Quorn mixture along with the tomato purée. Cover and simmer gently for about 45 minutes, adding the remaining stock as necessary.

Meanwhile, bring a large pan of salted water to the boil and add the spaghetti. Cook until *al dente* or according to the packet instructions. Drain well. Remove the sauce from the heat, add the crème fraîche and season to taste with salt and pepper. Stir in the parsley and serve immediately with the pasta.

 Try This: FOR AN ALTERNATIVE: 272   FOR PUDDING: 352

Ratatouille & Pasta Bake

SERVES 4

1 tbsp olive oil
2 large onions, peeled and
   finely chopped
400 g can chopped tomatoes
100 ml/3½ fl oz white wine
½ tsp caster sugar
salt and freshly ground black
   pepper
40 g/1½ oz butter

2 garlic cloves, peeled and
   crushed
125 g/4 oz mushrooms,
   wiped and thickly sliced
700 g/1½ lb courgettes,
   trimmed and thickly sliced
125 g/4 oz fresh spinach
   lasagne
2 large eggs

2 tbsp double cream
75 g/3 oz mozzarella cheese,
   grated
25 g/1 oz pecorino cheese,
   grated
green salad, to serve

Preheat the oven to 190°C/375°F/Gas Mark 5, 10 minutes before cooking. Heat the olive oil in a heavy-based pan, add half the onion and cook gently for 2–3 minutes. Stir in the tomatoes and wine, then simmer for 20 minutes, or until a thick consistency is formed. Add the sugar and season to taste with salt and pepper. Reserve.

Meanwhile, melt the butter in another pan, add the remaining onion, the garlic, mushrooms and courgettes and cook for 10 minutes, or until softened.

Spread a little tomato sauce in the base of a lightly oiled, 1.4 litre/2 ½ pint baking dish. Top with a layer of lasagne and spoon over half the mushroom and courgette mixture. Repeat the layers, finishing with a layer of lasagne.

Beat the eggs and cream together, then pour over the lasagne. Mix the mozzarella and pecorino cheeses together then sprinkle on top of the lasagne. Place in the preheated oven and cook for 20 minutes, or until golden-brown. Serve immediately with a green salad.

 Try This: FOR AN ALTERNATIVE: 268   FOR PUDDING: 364

Spring Vegetable & Herb Risotto

Serves 2–3

1 litre/1¾ pint
  vegetable stock
125 g/4 oz asparagus
  tips, trimmed
125 g/4 oz baby
  carrots, scrubbed
50 g/2 oz peas, fresh or
  frozen

50 g/2 oz fine French
  beans, trimmed
1 tbsp olive oil
1 onion, peeled and
  finely chopped
1 garlic clove, peeled and
  finely chopped
2 tsp freshly chopped thyme

225 g/8 oz risotto rice
150 ml/¼ pint white wine
1 tbsp each freshly chopped
  basil, chives and parsley
zest of ½ lemon
3 tbsp half-fat crème fraîche
salt and freshly ground
  black pepper

Bring the vegetable stock to the boil in a large saucepan and add the asparagus, baby carrots, peas and beans. Bring the stock back to the boil and remove the vegetables at once using a slotted spoon. Rinse under cold running water. Drain again and reserve. Keep the stock hot.

Heat the oil in a large deep frying pan and add the onion. Cook over a medium heat for 4–5 minutes until starting to brown. Add the garlic and thyme and cook for a further few seconds. Add the rice and stir well for a minute until the rice is hot and coated in oil.

Add the white wine and stir constantly until the wine is almost completely absorbed by the rice. Begin adding the stock a ladleful at a time, stirring well and waiting until the last ladleful has been absorbed before stirring in the next. Add the vegetables after using about half of the stock. Continue until all the stock is used. This will take 20–25 minutes. The rice and vegetables should both be tender.

Remove the pan from the heat. Stir in the herbs, lemon zest and crème fraîche. Season to taste with salt and pepper and serve immediately.

Roasted Butternut Squash

SERVES 4

2 small butternut squash
4 garlic cloves, peeled
   and crushed
1 tbsp olive oil
salt and freshly ground
   black pepper
1 tbsp walnut oil
4 medium-sized leeks,

trimmed, cleaned and
   thinly sliced
1 tbsp black mustard seeds
300 g can cannellini beans,
   drained and rinsed
125 g/4 oz fine French
   beans, halved
150 ml/¼ pint vegetable stock

50 g/2 oz rocket
2 tbsp freshly snipped chives
fresh chives, to garnish

To serve:
4 tbsp low-fat fromage frais
mixed salad

Preheat the oven to 200°C/400°F/Gas Mark 6. Cut the butternut squash in half lengthwise and scoop out all of the seeds.

Score the squash in a diamond pattern with a sharp knife. Mix the garlic with the olive oil and brush over the cut surfaces of the squash. Season well with salt and pepper. Put on a baking sheet and roast for 40 minutes until tender.

Heat the walnut oil in a saucepan and fry the leeks and mustard seeds for 5 minutes.

Add the drained cannellini beans, French beans and vegetable stock. Bring to the boil and simmer gently for 5 minutes until the French beans are tender.

Remove from the heat and stir in the rocket and chives. Season well. Remove the squash from the oven and allow to cool for 5 minutes. Spoon in the bean mixture. Garnish with a few snipped chives and serve immediately with the fromage frais and a mixed salad.

Try This: FOR AN ALTERNATIVE: 284 FOR PUDDING: 306

Mushroom Stew

SERVES 4

15 g/½ oz dried
   porcini mushrooms
900 g/2 lb assorted fresh
   mushrooms, wiped
2 tbsp good-quality
   virgin olive oil
1 onion, peeled and
   finely chopped

2 garlic cloves, peeled and
   finely chopped
1 tbsp fresh thyme leaves
pinch of ground cloves
salt and freshly ground
   black pepper
700 g/1½ lb tomatoes,
   peeled, deseeded

   and chopped
225 g/8 oz instant polenta
600ml/1 pint vegetable stock
3 tbsp freshly chopped
   mixed herbs
sprigs of parsley, to garnish

Soak the porcini mushrooms in a small bowl of hot water for 20 minutes. Drain reserving the porcini mushrooms and their soaking liquor. Cut the fresh mushrooms in half and reserve.

In a saucepan, heat the oil and add the onion. Cook gently for 5–7 minutes until softened. Add the garlic, thyme and cloves and continue cooking for 2 minutes.

Add all the mushrooms and cook for 8–10 minutes until the mushrooms have softened, stirring often. Season to taste with salt and pepper and add the tomatoes and the reserved soaking liquid.

Simmer, partly-covered, over a low heat for about 20 minutes until thickened. Adjust the seasoning to taste.

Meanwhile, cook the polenta according to the packet instructions using the vegetable stock. Stir in the herbs and divide between 4 dishes.

Ladle the mushrooms over the polenta, garnish with the parsley and serve immediately.

Beetroot & Potato Medley

SERVES 4

350 g/12 oz raw
   baby beetroot
½ tsp sunflower oil
225 g/8 oz new potatoes
½ cucumber, peeled

3 tbsp white wine vinegar
150 ml/5 fl oz natural
   low-fat yogurt
salt and freshly ground
   black pepper

fresh salad leaves
1 tbsp freshly snipped
   chives, to garnish

Preheat the oven to 180°C/350°F/Gas Mark 4. Scrub the beetroot thoroughly and place on a baking tray. Brush the beetroot with a little oil and cook for 1½ hours or until a skewer is easily insertable into the beetroot. Allow to cool a little, then remove the skins.

Cook the potatoes in boiling water for about 10 minutes. Rinse in cold water and drain. Reserve the potatoes until cool. Dice evenly.

Cut the cucumber into cubes and place in a mixing bowl. Chop the beetroot into small cubes and add to the bowl with the reserved potatoes. Gently mix the vegetables together.

Mix together the vinegar and yogurt and season to taste with a little salt and pepper. Pour over the vegetables and combine gently.

Arrange on a bed of salad leaves garnished with the snipped chives and serve.

Try This: FOR AN ALTERNATIVE: 292 FOR PUDDING: 324

Vegetarian Cassoulet

SERVES 4

225 g/8 oz dried haricot
  beans, soaked overnight
2 medium onions
1 bay leaf
1.4 litres/2½ pints cold water
550 g/1¼ lb large potatoes,
  peeled and cut into 1 cm/
  ½ inch slices
salt and freshly ground

black pepper
5 tsp olive oil
1 large garlic clove, peeled
  and crushed
2 leeks, trimmed and sliced
200 g can chopped tomatoes
1 tsp dark muscovado sugar
1 tbsp freshly chopped
  thyme

2 tbsp freshly chopped parsley
3 courgettes, trimmed and
  sliced

For the topping:
50 g/2 oz fresh white
  breadcrumbs
25 g/1oz Cheddar cheese,
  finely grated

Preheat the oven to 180°C/350°F/Gas Mark 4, 10 minutes before required. Drain the beans, rinse under cold running water and put in a saucepan. Peel 1 of the onions and add to the beans with the bay leaf. Pour in the water. Bring to a rapid boil and cook for 10 minutes, then turn down the heat, cover and simmer for 50 minutes, or until the beans are almost tender. Drain the beans, reserving the liquor, but discarding the onion and bay leaf.

Cook the potatoes in a saucepan of lightly salted boiling water for 6–7 minutes until almost tender when tested with the point of a knife. Drain and reserve.

Peel and chop the remaining onion. Heat the oil in a frying pan and cook the onion with the garlic and leeks for 10 minutes until softened. Stir in the tomatoes, sugar, thyme and parsley. Stir in the beans, with 300 ml/½ pint of the reserved liquor and season to taste. Simmer, uncovered, for 5 minutes.

Layer the potato slices, courgettes and ladlefuls of the bean mixture in a large flameproof casserole. To make the topping, mix together the breadcrumbs and cheese and sprinkle over the top. Bake in the preheated oven for 40 minutes, or until the vegetables are cooked through and the topping is golden brown and crisp. Serve immediately.

Try This: FOR AN ALTERNATIVE: 272   FOR PUDDING: 302

Sweet Potato Cakes with Mango & Tomato Salsa

SERVES 4

700 g/1½ lb sweet potatoes, peeled and cut into large chunks

salt and freshly ground black pepper

25 g/1 oz butter

1 onion, peeled and chopped

1 garlic clove, peeled and crushed

pinch of freshly grated nutmeg

1 medium egg, beaten

50 g/2 oz quick-cook polenta

2 tbsp sunflower oil

For the salsa:

1 ripe mango, peeled, stoned and diced

6 cherry tomatoes, cut in wedges

4 spring onions, trimmed and thinly sliced

1 red chilli, deseeded and finely chopped

finely grated rind and juice of ½ lime

2 tbsp freshly chopped mint

1 tsp clear honey

salad leaves, to serve

Steam or cook the sweet potatoes in lightly salted boiling water for 15–20 minutes, until tender. Drain well, then mash until smooth.

Melt the butter in a saucepan. Add the onion and garlic and cook gently for 10 minutes until soft. Add to the mashed sweet potato and season with the nutmeg, salt and pepper. Stir together until mixed thoroughly. Leave to cool.

Shape the mixture into 4 oval potato cakes, about 2.5 cm/1 inch thick. Dip first in the beaten egg, allowing the excess to fall back into the bowl, then coat in the polenta. Refrigerate for at least 30 minutes.

Meanwhile, mix together all the ingredients for the salsa. Spoon into a serving bowl, cover with clingfilm and leave at room temperature to allow the flavours to develop.

Heat the oil in a frying pan and cook the potato cakes for 4–5 minutes on each side. Serve with the salsa and salad leaves.

Try This: FOR AN ALTERNATIVE: 276   FOR PUDDING: 368

Thai–style Cauliflower & Potato Curry

SERVES 4

450 g/1 lb new potatoes, peeled and halved or quartered
350 g/12 oz cauliflower florets
3 garlic cloves, peeled and crushed
1 onion, peeled and finely chopped

40 g/1½ oz ground almonds
1 tsp ground coriander
½ tsp ground cumin
½ tsp turmeric
3 tbsp groundnut oil
salt and freshly ground black pepper
50 g/2 oz creamed coconut,

broken into small pieces
200 ml/7 fl oz vegetable stock
1 tbsp mango chutney
sprigs of fresh coriander, to garnish
freshly cooked long-grain rice, to serve

Bring a saucepan of lightly salted water to the boil, add the potatoes and cook for 15 minutes or until just tender. Drain and leave to cool. Boil the cauliflower for 2 minutes, then drain and refresh under cold running water. Drain again and reserve.

Meanwhile, blend the garlic, onion, ground almonds and spices with 2 tablespoons of the oil and salt and pepper to taste in a food processor until a smooth paste is formed. Heat a wok, add the remaining oil and when hot, add the spice paste and cook for 3–4 minutes, stirring continuously.

Dissolve the creamed coconut in 6 tablespoons of boiling water and add to the wok. Pour in the stock, cook for 2–3 minutes, then stir in the cooked potatoes and cauliflower.

Stir in the mango chutney and heat through for 3–4 minutes or until piping hot. Tip into a warmed serving dish, garnish with sprigs of fresh coriander and serve immediately with freshly cooked rice.

Try This: FOR AN ALTERNATIVE: 284 FOR PUDDING: 316

Cheese & Onion Oat Pie

SERVES 4

1 tbsp sunflower oil, plus 1 tsp
25 g/1 oz butter
2 medium onions, peeled and sliced
1 garlic clove, peeled and crushed

150 g/5 oz porridge oats
125 g/4 oz mature Cheddar cheese, grated
2 medium eggs, lightly beaten
2 tbsp freshly chopped

parsley
salt and freshly ground black pepper
275 g/10 oz baking potato, peeled

Preheat the oven to 180°C/350°F/Gas Mark 4. Heat the oil and half the butter in a saucepan until melted. Add the onions and garlic and gently cook for 10 minutes, or until soft. Remove from the heat and tip into a large bowl.

Spread the oats out on a baking sheet and toast in the hot oven for 12 minutes. Leave to cool, then add to the onions with the cheese, eggs and parsley. Season to taste with salt and pepper and mix well.

Line the base of a 20.5 cm/8 inch round sandwich tin with greaseproof paper and oil well. Thinly slice the potato and arrange the slices on the base, overlapping them slightly. Spoon the cheese and oat mixture on top of the potato, spreading evenly with the back of a spoon. Cover with tinfoil and bake for 30 minutes.

Invert the pie onto a baking sheet so that the potatoes are on top. Carefully remove the tin and lining paper.

Preheat the grill to medium. Melt the remaining butter and carefully brush over the potato topping. Cook under the preheated grill for 5–6 minutes until the potatoes are lightly browned. Cut into wedges and serve.

Try This: FOR AN ALTERNATIVE: 290   FOR PUDDING: 342

Layered Cheese & Herb Potato Cake

SERVES 4

900 g/2 lb waxy potatoes
3 tbsp freshly snipped chives
2 tbsp freshly chopped parsley
225 g/8 oz mature Cheddar cheese

2 large egg yolks
1 tsp paprika
125 g/4 oz fresh white breadcrumbs
50 g/2 oz almonds, toasted and roughly chopped

salt and freshly ground black pepper
50 g/2 oz butter, melted
mixed salad or steamed vegetables, to serve

Preheat the oven to 180°C/350°F/Gas Mark 4. Lightly oil and line the base of a 20.5 cm/8 inch round cake tin with lightly oiled greaseproof or baking parchment paper. Peel and thinly slice the potatoes and reserve. Stir the chives, parsley, cheese and egg yolks together in a small bowl and reserve. Mix the paprika into the breadcrumbs.

Sprinkle the almonds over the base of the lined tin. Cover with half the potatoes, arranging them in layers, then sprinkle with the paprika breadcrumb mixture and season to taste with salt and pepper.

Spoon the cheese and herb mixture over the breadcrumbs with a little more seasoning, then arrange the remaining potatoes on top. Drizzle over the melted butter and press the surface down firmly.

Bake in the preheated oven for 1¼ hours, or until golden and cooked through. Let the tin stand for 10 minutes before carefully turning out and serving in thick wedges. Serve immediately with salad or freshly cooked vegetables.

Try This: FOR AN ALTERNATIVE: 288   FOR PUDDING: 300

Chunky Vegetable & Fennel Goulash with Dumplings

SERVES 4

2 fennel bulbs, weighing
  about 450 g/1 lb
2 tbsp sunflower oil
1 large onion, peeled
  and sliced
1½ tbsp paprika
1 tbsp plain flour
300 ml/½ pint vegetable
  stock

400 g can chopped
  tomatoes
450 g/1 lb potatoes,
  peeled and cut into 2.5
  cm/1 inch chunks
125 g/4 oz small button
  mushrooms
salt and freshly ground
  black pepper

For the dumplings:
1 tbsp sunflower oil
1 small onion, peeled and
  finely chopped
1 medium egg
3 tbsp milk
3 tbsp freshly chopped parsley
125 g/4 oz fresh white
  breadcrumbs

Cut the fennel bulbs in half widthways. Thickly slice the stalks and cut the bulbs into 8 wedges. Heat the oil in a large saucepan or flameproof casserole. Add the onion and fennel and cook gently for 10 minutes until soft. Stir in the paprika and flour.

Remove from the heat and gradually stir in the stock. Add the chopped tomatoes, potatoes and mushrooms. Season to taste with salt and pepper. Bring to the boil, reduce the heat and simmer for 20 minutes.

Meanwhile, make the dumplings. Heat the oil in a frying pan and gently cook the onion for 10 minutes, until soft. Leave to cool for a few minutes. In a bowl, beat the egg and milk together, then add the onion, parsley, breadcrumbs, and season to taste. With damp hands form the breadcrumb mixture into 12 round dumplings each about the size of a walnut.

Arrange the dumplings on top of the goulash. Cover and cook for a further 15 minutes, until the dumplings are cooked and the vegetables are tender. Serve immediately.

Try This: FOR AN ALTERNATIVE: 282   FOR PUDDING: 298

Sweet Pies & Puddings

Crunchy Rhubarb Crumble

SERVES 6

125 g/4 oz plain flour	50 g/2 oz demerara sugar	450 g/1 lb fresh rhubarb
50 g/2 oz softened butter	1 tbsp sesame seeds	50 g/2 oz caster sugar
50 g/2 oz rolled oats	½ tsp ground cinnamon	custard or cream, to serve

Preheat the oven to 180°C/350°F/Gas Mark 4. Place the flour in a large bowl and cut the butter into cubes. Add to the flour and rub in with the fingertips until the mixture looks like fine breadcrumbs, or blend for a few seconds in a food processor.

Stir in the rolled oats, demerara sugar, sesame seeds and cinnamon. Mix well and reserve.

Prepare the rhubarb by removing the thick ends of the stalks and cut diagonally into 2.5 cm/1 inch chunks. Wash thoroughly and pat dry with a clean tea towel. Place the rhubarb in a 1.1 litre/ 2 pint pie dish.

Sprinkle the caster sugar over the rhubarb and top with the reserved crumble mixture. Level the top of the crumble so that all the fruit is well covered and press down firmly. If liked, sprinkle the top with a little extra caster sugar.

Place on a baking sheet and bake in the preheated oven for 40–50 minutes, or until the fruit is soft and the topping is golden brown. Sprinkle the pudding with some more caster sugar and serve hot with custard or cream.

Try This: FOR AN ALTERNATIVE: 310 FOR A MAIN MEAL: 218

Baked Apple Dumplings

SERVES 4

225 g/8 oz self-raising flour	4 medium cooking apples	2 tsp caster sugar
¼ tsp salt	4–6 tsp luxury mincemeat	custard or vanilla sauce, to
125 g/4 oz shredded suet	1 medium egg white, beaten	serve

Preheat the oven to 200°C/400°F/Gas Mark 6. Lightly oil a baking tray. Place the flour and salt in a bowl and stir in the suet. Add just enough water to the mixture to mix to a soft but not sticky dough, using the fingertips.

Turn the dough on to a lightly floured board and knead lightly into a ball. Divide the dough into 4 pieces and roll out each piece into a thin square, large enough to encase the apples.

Peel and core the apples and place 1 apple in the centre of each square of pastry.

Fill the centre of the apple with mincemeat, brush the edges of each pastry square with water and draw the corners up to meet over each apple. Press the edges of the pastry firmly together and decorate with pastry leaves and shapes made from the extra pastry trimmings.

Place the apples on the prepared baking tray, brush with the egg white and sprinkle with the sugar.

Bake in the preheated oven for 30 minutes or until golden and the pastry and apples are cooked. Serve the dumplings hot with the custard or vanilla sauce.

Try This: FOR AN ALTERNATIVE: 304 FOR A MAIN MEAL: 178

Jam Roly Poly

SERVES 6

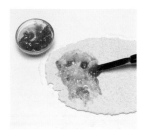

225 g/8 oz self-raising flour	about 150 ml/¼ pint water	1 tsp caster sugar
¼ tsp salt	3 tbsp strawberry jam	ready-made jam sauce, to
125 g/4 oz shredded suet	1 tbsp milk, to glaze	serve

Preheat the oven to 200°C/400°F/Gas Mark 6. Make the pastry by sifting the flour and salt into a large bowl. Add the suet and mix lightly, then add the water a little at a time and mix to form a soft and pliable dough. (Take care not to make the dough too wet.)

Turn the dough out on to a lightly floured board and knead gently until smooth. Roll the dough out into a 23 cm/9 inch x 28 cm/11 inch rectangle.

Spread the jam over the pastry leaving a border of 1 cm/½ inch all round. Fold the border over the jam and brush the edges with water.

Lightly roll the rectangle up from one of the short sides, seal the top edge and press the ends together. (Do not roll the pudding up too tightly.)

Turn the pudding upside down on to a large piece of greaseproof paper large enough to come halfway up the sides. (If using non-stick paper, then oil lightly.) Tie the ends of the paper, to make a boat-shaped paper case for the pudding to sit in and to leave plenty of room for the roly poly to expand.

Brush the pudding lightly with milk and sprinkle with the sugar. Bake in the preheated oven for 30–40 minutes, or until well risen and golden. Serve immediately with the jam sauce.

Try This: FOR AN ALTERNATIVE: 326   FOR A MAIN MEAL: 164

Queen of Puddings

SERVES 4

75 g/3 oz fresh white breadcrumbs	450 ml/¾ pint full-cream milk	2 medium eggs, separated
25 g/1 oz granulated sugar	25 g/1 oz butter	2 tbsp seedless raspberry jam
	grated rind of 1 small lemon	50 g/2 oz caster sugar

Preheat the oven to 170°C/325°F/Gas Mark 3. Oil a 900 ml/1½ pint ovenproof baking dish and reserve.

Mix the breadcrumbs and sugar together in a bowl.

Pour the milk into a small saucepan and heat gently with the butter and lemon rind until the butter has melted. Allow the mixture to cool a little, then pour over the breadcrumbs. Stir well and leave to soak for 30 minutes.

Whisk the egg yolks into the cooled breadcrumb mixture and pour into the prepared dish. Place the dish on a baking sheet and bake in the preheated oven for about 30 minutes, or until firm and set. Remove from the oven.

Allow to cool slightly, then spread the jam over the pudding. Whisk the egg whites until stiff and standing in peaks. Gently fold in the caster sugar with a metal spoon or rubber spatula. Pile the meringue over the top of the pudding.

Return the dish to the oven for a further 25–30 minutes, or until the meringue is crisp and just slightly coloured. Serve hot or cold.

Try This: FOR AN ALTERNATIVE: 324 FOR A MAIN MEAL: 98

Eve's Pudding

SERVES 6

450 g/1 lb cooking apples
175 g/6 oz blackberries
75 g/3 oz demerara sugar
grated rind of 1 lemon

125 g/4 oz caster sugar
125 g/4 oz butter
few drops of vanilla essence
2 medium eggs, beaten

125 g/4 oz self-raising flour
1 tbsp icing sugar
ready-made custard, to
    serve

Preheat the oven to 180°C/350°F/Gas Mark 4. Oil a 1.1 litre/2 pint baking dish.

Peel, core and slice the apples and place a layer in the base of the prepared dish. Sprinkle over some of the blackberries, a little demerara sugar and lemon zest. Continue to layer the apple and blackberries in this way until all the ingredients have been used.

Cream the sugar and butter together until light and fluffy. Beat in the vanilla essence and then the eggs a little at a time, adding a spoonful of flour after each addition. Fold in the extra flour with a metal spoon or rubber spatula and mix well.

Spread the sponge mixture over the top of the fruit and level with the back of a spoon.

Place the dish on a baking sheet and bake in the preheated oven for 35–40 minutes, or until well risen and golden brown. (To test if the pudding is cooked, press the cooked sponge lightly with a clean finger – if it springs back the sponge is cooked.)

Dust the pudding with a little icing sugar and serve immediately with the custard.

Try This: FOR AN ALTERNATIVE: 298   FOR A MAIN MEAL: 184

Rice Pudding

SERVES 4

60 g/2½ oz pudding rice
50 g/2 oz granulated sugar
410 g can light
    evaporated milk

300 ml/½ pint semi-
    skimmed milk
pinch of freshly
    grated nutmeg

25 g/1 oz half-fat butter
reduced sugar jam,
    to decorate

Preheat the oven to 150°C/300°F/Gas Mark 2. Lightly oil a large ovenproof dish.

Sprinkle the rice and the sugar into the dish and mix.

Bring the evaporated milk and milk to the boil in a small pan, stirring occasionally. Stir the milks into the rice and mix well until the rice is coated thoroughly. Sprinkle over the nutmeg, cover with tinfoil and bake in the preheated oven for 30 minutes.

Remove the pudding from the oven and stir well, breaking up any lumps. Cover with the same tinfoil. Bake in the preheated oven for a further 30 minutes. Remove from the oven and stir well again. Dot the pudding with butter and bake for a further 45–60 minutes, until the rice is tender and the skin is browned.

Divide the pudding into 4 individual serving bowls. Top with a large spoonful of the jam and serve immediately.

Try This: FOR AN ALTERNATIVE: 300   FOR A MAIN MEAL: 66

College Pudding

SERVES 4

125 g/4 oz shredded suet
125 g/4 oz fresh
   white breadcrumbs
50 g/2 oz sultanas
50 g/2 oz seedless raisins

½ tsp ground cinnamon
¼ tsp freshly grated nutmeg
¼ tsp mixed spice
50 g/2 oz caster sugar
½ tsp baking powder

2 medium eggs, beaten
orange zest, to garnish

Preheat the oven to 180°C/350°F/Gas Mark 4. Lightly oil an ovenproof 900 ml/1½ pint ovenproof pudding basin and place a small circle of greaseproof paper in the base.

Mix the shredded suet and breadcrumbs together and rub lightly together with the fingertips to remove any lumps.

Stir in the dried fruit, spices, sugar and baking powder. Add the eggs and beat lightly together until the mixture is well blended and the fruit is evenly distributed.

Spoon the mixture into the prepared pudding basin and level the surface. Place on a baking tray and cover lightly with some greaseproof paper.

Bake in the preheated oven for 20 minutes, then remove the paper and continue to bake for a further 10–15 minutes, or until the top is firm.

When the pudding is cooked, remove from the oven and carefully turn out on to a warmed serving dish. Decorate with the orange zest and serve immediately.

Try This: FOR AN ALTERNATIVE: 312 FOR A MAIN MEAL: 226

Oaty Fruit Puddings

SERVES 4

125 g/4 oz rolled oats
50 g/2 oz low-fat
  spread, melted
2 tbsp chopped almonds
1 tbsp clear honey

pinch of ground cinnamon
2 pears, peeled, cored and
  finely chopped
1 tbsp marmalade
orange zest, to decorate

low-fat custard or fruit-
  flavoured low-fat yogurt,
  to serve

Preheat the oven to 200°C/400°F/Gas Mark 6. Lightly oil and line the bases of 4 individual pudding bowls or muffin tins with a small circle of greaseproof paper.

Mix together the oats, low-fat spread, nuts, honey and cinnamon in a small bowl.

Using a spoon, spread two thirds of the oaty mixture over the base and around the sides of the pudding bowls or muffin tins.

Toss together the pears and marmalade and spoon into the oaty cases. Scatter over the remaining oaty mixture to cover the pears and marmalade.

Bake in the preheated oven for 15–20 minutes, until cooked and the tops of the puddings are golden and crisp.

Leave for 5 minutes before removing the pudding bowls or the muffin tins. Decorate with orange zest and serve hot with low-fat custard or low-fat fruit-flavoured yogurt.

Try This: FOR AN ALTERNATIVE: 296 FOR A MAIN MEAL: 122

Cherry Batter Pudding

SERVES 4

450 g/1 lb fresh cherries (or
   425 g can pitted cherries)
50 g/2 oz plain flour
pinch of salt

3 tbsp caster sugar
2 medium eggs
300 ml/½ pint milk
40 g/1½ oz butter

1 tbsp rum
extra caster sugar, to dredge
fresh cream, to serve

Preheat the oven to 220°C/425°F/Gas Mark 7. Lightly oil a 900 ml/1½ pint shallow baking dish.

Rinse the cherries, drain well and remove the stones (using a cherry stoner if possible). If using canned cherries, drain well, discard the juice and place in the prepared dish.

Sift the flour and salt into a large bowl. Stir in 2 tablespoons of the caster sugar and make a well in the centre. Beat the eggs, then pour into the well of the dry ingredients.

Warm the milk and slowly pour into the well, beating throughout and gradually drawing in the flour from the sides of the bowl. Continue until a smooth batter has formed.

Melt the butter in a small saucepan over a low heat, then stir into the batter with the rum. Reserve for 15 minutes, then beat again until smooth and easy to pour.

Pour into the prepared baking dish and bake in the preheated oven for 30–35 minutes, or until golden brown and set.

Remove the pudding from the oven, sprinkle with the remaining sugar and serve hot with plenty of fresh cream.

Try This: FOR AN ALTERNATIVE: 308 FOR A MAIN MEAL: 178

Lemon & Apricot Pudding

SERVES 4

125 g/4 oz ready-to-eat
  dried apricots
3 tbsp orange juice, warmed
50 g/2 oz butter

125 g/4 oz caster sugar
juice and grated rind of 2
  lemons
2 medium eggs

50 g/2 oz self-raising flour
300 ml/½ pint milk
custard or fresh cream, to
  serve

Preheat the oven to 180°C/350°F/Gas Mark 4. Oil a 1.1 litre/2 pint pie dish.

Soak the apricots in the orange juice for 10–15 minutes or until most of the juice has been absorbed, then place in the base of the pie dish.

Cream the butter and sugar together with the lemon rind until light and fluffy.

Separate the eggs. Beat the egg yolks into the creamed mixture with a spoonful of flour after each addition. Add the remaining flour and beat well until smooth.

Stir the milk and lemon juice into the creamed mixture. Whisk the egg whites in a grease-free mixing bowl until stiff and standing in peaks. Fold into the mixture using a metal spoon or rubber spatula.

Pour into the prepared dish and place in a baking tray filled with enough cold water to come halfway up the sides of the dish. Bake in the preheated oven for about 45 minutes, or until the sponge is firm and golden brown. Remove from the oven. Serve immediately with the custard or fresh cream.

Try This: FOR AN ALTERNATIVE: 316   FOR A MAIN MEAL: 80

Summer Pudding

SERVES 4

450 g/1 lb redcurrants
125 g/4 oz caster sugar
350 g/12 oz strawberries,
  hulled and halved
125 g/4 oz raspberries

2 tbsp Grand Marnier
  or Cointreau
8–10 medium slices white
  bread, crusts removed
mint sprigs, to decorate

low-fat Greek-set yogurt or
  low-fat fromage frais,
  to serve

Place the redcurrants, sugar and 1 tablespoon of water in a large saucepan. Heat gently until the sugar has just dissolved and the juices have just begun to run.

Remove the saucepan from the heat and stir in the strawberries, raspberries and the Grand Marnier or Cointreau.

Line the base and sides of a 1.1 litre/2 pint pudding basin with two thirds of the bread, making sure that the slices overlap each other slightly.

Spoon the fruit with their juices into the bread-lined pudding basin, then top with the remaining bread slices.

Place a small plate on top of the pudding inside the pudding basin. Ensure the plate fits tightly, then weigh down with a clean can or some weights and chill in the refrigerator overnight.

When ready to serve, remove the weights and plate. Carefully loosen round the sides of the basin with a round-bladed knife. Invert the pudding on to a serving plate, decorate with the mint sprigs and serve with the yogurt or fromage frais.

Try This: FOR AN ALTERNATIVE: 328 FOR A MAIN MEAL: 72

Creamy Puddings with Mixed Berry Compote

SERVES 6

300 ml/½ pint half-fat double cream
1 x 250 g carton ricotta cheese

50 g/2 oz caster sugar
125 g/4 oz white chocolate, broken into pieces
350 g/12 oz mixed summer

fruits such as strawberries, blueberries and raspberries
2 tbsp Cointreau

Set the freezer to rapid freeze. Whip the cream until soft peaks form. Fold in the ricotta cheese and half the sugar.

Place the chocolate in a bowl set over a saucepan of simmering water. Stir until melted. Remove from the heat and leave to cool, stirring occasionally. Stir into the cheese mixture until well blended.

Spoon the mixture into 6 individual pudding moulds and level the surface of each pudding with the back of a spoon. Place in the freezer and freeze for 4 hours.

Place the fruits and the remaining sugar in a pan and heat gently, stirring occasionally until the sugar has dissolved and the juices are just beginning to run. Stir in the Cointreau to taste.

Dip the pudding moulds in hot water for 30 seconds and invert on to 6 serving plates. Spoon the fruit compote over the puddings and serve immediately. Remember to return the freezer to its normal setting.

Try This: FOR AN ALTERNATIVE: 320 FOR A MAIN MEAL: 248

Vanilla & Lemon
Panna Cotta with Raspberry Sauce

SERVES 6

900 ml/1½ pints double
    cream
1 vanilla pod, split
100 g/3½ oz caster sugar

zest of 1 lemon
3 sheets gelatine
5 tbsp milk
450 g/1 lb raspberries

3–4 tbsp icing sugar, to taste
1 tbsp lemon juice
extra lemon zest, to decorate

Put the cream, vanilla pod and sugar into a saucepan. Bring to the boil, then simmer for 10 minutes until slightly reduced, stirring to prevent scalding. Remove from the heat, stir in the lemon zest and remove the vanilla pod.

Soak the gelatine in the milk for 5 minutes, or until softened. Squeeze out any excess milk and add to the hot cream. Stir well until dissolved.

Pour the cream mixture into 6 ramekins or mini pudding moulds and leave in the refrigerator for 4 hours, or until set.

Meanwhile, put 175 g/6 oz of the raspberries in a food processor with the icing sugar and lemon juice. Blend to a purée then pass the mixture through a sieve. Fold in the remaining raspberries with a metal spoon or rubber spatula and chill in the refrigerator until ready to serve.

To serve, dip each of the moulds into hot water for a few seconds, then turn out on to 6 individual serving plates. Spoon some of the raspberry sauce over and around the panna cotta, decorate with extra lemon zest and serve.

Autumn Fruit Layer

SERVES 4

450 g/1 lb Bramley
   cooking apples
225 g/8 oz blackberries
50 g/2 oz soft brown sugar
juice of 1 lemon

50 g/2 oz low-fat spread
200 g/7 oz breadcrumbs
225 g/8 oz honey-coated nut
   mix, chopped
redcurrants and mint leaves,

to decorate
half-fat whipped cream or
   reduced-fat ice cream,
   to serve

Peel, core and slice the cooking apples and place in a saucepan with the blackberries, sugar and lemon juice. Cover the fruit mixture and simmer, stirring occasionally for about 15 minutes or until the apples and blackberries have formed into a thick purée. Remove the pan from the heat and allow to cool.

Melt the low-fat spread in a frying pan and cook the breadcrumbs for 5–10 minutes, stirring occasionally until golden and crisp. Remove the pan from the heat and stir in the nuts. Allow to cool.

Alternately layer the fruit purée and breadcrumbs into 4 tall glasses. Store the desserts in the refrigerator to chill and remove when ready to serve.

Decorate with redcurrants and mint leaves and serve with half-fat whipped cream or a reduced-fat vanilla or raspberry ice cream.

Summer Pavlova

SERVES 6–8

4 medium egg whites
225 g/8 oz caster sugar
1 tsp vanilla essence
2 tsp white wine vinegar
1½ tsp cornflour

300 ml/½ pint half-fat
  Greek-set yogurt
2 tbsp honey
225 g/8 oz strawberries,
  hulled

125 g/4 oz raspberries
125 g/4 oz blueberries
4 kiwis, peeled and sliced
icing sugar, to decorate

Preheat the oven to 150°C/300°F/Gas Mark 2. Line a baking sheet with a sheet of greaseproof or baking parchment paper.

Place the egg whites in a clean grease-free bowl and whisk until very stiff. Whisk in half the sugar, vanilla essence, vinegar and cornflour, continue whisking until stiff. Gradually, whisk in the remaining sugar, a teaspoonful at a time until very stiff and glossy.

Using a large spoon, arrange spoonfuls of the meringue in a circle on the greaseproof paper or baking parchment paper. Bake in the preheated oven for 1 hour until crisp and dry. Turn the oven off and leave the meringue in the oven to cool completely.

Remove the meringue from the baking sheet and peel away the parchment paper. Mix together the yogurt and honey. Place the pavlova on a serving plate and spoon the yogurt into the centre.

Scatter over the strawberries, raspberries, blueberries and kiwis. Dust with the icing sugar and serve

Try This: FOR AN ALTERNATIVE: 316   FOR A MAIN MEAL: 70

Fruity Roulade

SERVES 4

For the sponge:
3 medium eggs
75 g/3 oz caster sugar
75 g/3 oz plain flour, sieved
1–2 tbsp caster sugar
    for sprinkling

For the filling:
125 g/4 oz Quark
125 g/4 oz half-fat
    Greek yogurt
25 g/1 oz caster sugar
1 tbsp orange
    liqueur (optional)

grated rind of 1 orange
125 g/4 oz strawberries,
    hulled and cut into quarters

To decorate:
strawberries
sifted icing sugar

Preheat the oven to 220°C/425°F/Gas Mark 7. Lightly oil and line a 33 x 23 cm/13 x 9 inch Swiss roll tin with greaseproof or baking parchment paper.

Using an electric whisk, whisk the eggs and sugar until the mixture is double in volume and leaves a trail across the top. Fold in the flour with a metal spoon or rubber spatula. Pour into the prepared tin and bake in the preheated oven for 10–12 minutes, until well risen and golden.

Place a whole sheet of greaseproof or baking parchment paper out on a flat work surface and sprinkle evenly with caster sugar.

Turn the cooked sponge out on to the paper, discard the paper, trim the sponge and roll up encasing the paper inside. Reserve until cool.

To make the filling, mix together the Quark, yogurt, caster sugar, liqueur (if using) and orange rind. Unroll the roulade and spread over the mixture. Scatter over the strawberries and roll up.

Decorate the roulade with the strawberries. Dust with the icing sugar and serve.

Try This: FOR AN ALTERNATIVE: 300   FOR A MAIN MEAL: 180

Fresh Strawberry Sponge Cake

8–10 SERVINGS

175 g/6 oz unsalted
   butter, softened
175 g/6 oz caster sugar
1 tsp vanilla essence

3 large eggs, beaten
175 g/6 oz self-raising flour
150 ml/¼ pint double cream
2 tbsp icing sugar, sifted

225 g/8 oz fresh strawberries,
   hulled and chopped
few extra strawberries, to
   decorate

Preheat the oven to 190°C/375°F/Gas Mark 5, 10 minutes before baking. Lightly oil and line the bases of 2 x 20.5 cm/8 inch round cake tins with greaseproof or baking paper.

Using an electric whisk, beat the butter, sugar and vanilla essence until pale and fluffy. Gradually beat in the eggs a little at a time, beating well between each addition.

Sift half the flour over the mixture and using a metal spoon or rubber spatula gently fold into the mixture. Sift over the remaining flour and fold in until just blended.

Divide the mixture between the tins, spreading evenly. Gently smooth the surfaces with the back of a spoon. Bake in the centre of the preheated oven for 20–25 minutes, or until well risen and golden.

Remove and leave to cool before turning out on to a wire rack. Whip the cream with 1 tablespoon of the icing sugar until it forms soft peaks. Fold in the chopped strawberries.

Spread 1 cake layer evenly with the mixture and top with the second cake layer, rounded side up.

Thickly dust the cake with icing sugar and decorate with the reserved strawberries. Carefully slide on to a serving plate and serve.

Try This: FOR AN ALTERNATIVE: 326   FOR A MAIN MEAL: 82

Fruity Chocolate Bread Pudding

SERVES 4

175 g/6 oz plain dark chocolate
1 small fruit loaf
125 g/4 oz ready-to-eat dried

apricots, roughly chopped
450 ml/¾ pint single cream
300 ml/½ pint milk
1 tbsp caster sugar

3 medium eggs
3 tbsp demerara sugar, for sprinkling

Preheat the oven to 180°C/350°F/Gas Mark 4, 10 minutes before cooking. Lightly butter a shallow ovenproof dish. Break the chocolate into small pieces, then place in a heatproof bowl set over a saucepan of gently simmering water. Heat gently, stirring frequently, until the chocolate has melted and is smooth. Remove from the heat and leave for about 10 minutes or until the chocolate begins to thicken slightly.

Cut the fruit loaf into medium to thick slices, then spread with the melted chocolate. Leave until almost set, then cut each slice in half to form a triangle. Layer the chocolate-coated bread slices and the chopped apricots in the buttered ovenproof dish.

Stir the cream and the milk together, then stir in the caster sugar. Beat the eggs, then gradually beat in the cream and milk mixture. Beat thoroughly until well blended. Carefully pour over the bread slices and apricots and leave to stand for 30 minutes.

Sprinkle with the demerara sugar and place in a roasting tin half filled with boiling water. Cook in the preheated oven for 45 minutes, or until golden and the custard is lightly set. Serve immediately.

Try This: FOR AN ALTERNATIVE: 346   FOR A MAIN MEAL: 98

Nutty Date Pudding with Chocolate Sauce

SERVES 4

125 g/4 oz butter, softened
125 g/4 oz golden caster
 sugar
3 medium eggs, beaten
175 g/6 oz self-raising flour,
 sifted
50 g/2 oz plain dark
 chocolate, grated

3 tbsp milk
75 g/3 oz hazelnuts, roughly
 chopped
75 g/3 oz stoned dates,
 roughly chopped
chopped toasted hazelnuts,
 to serve

For the chocolate sauce:
50 g/2 oz unsalted butter
50 g/2 oz soft light brown
 sugar
50 g/2 oz plain dark
 chocolate, broken into
 pieces
125 ml/4 fl oz double cream

Lightly oil a 1.1 litre/2 pint pudding basin and line the base with a small circle of nonstick baking parchment. Cream the butter and sugar together in a large bowl until light and fluffy. Add the beaten eggs a little at a time, adding 1 tablespoon of the flour after each addition. When all the eggs have been added, stir in the remaining flour. Add the grated chocolate and mix in lightly, then stir in the milk together with the hazelnuts and dates. Stir lightly until mixed together well.

Spoon the mixture into the prepared pudding basin and level the surface. Cover with a double sheet of baking parchment with a pleat in the centre, allowing for expansion, then cover either with a pudding cloth or a double sheet of tinfoil, again with a central pleat. Secure with string. Place in the top of a steamer, set over a saucepan of gently simmering water and steam for 2 hours, or until cooked and firm to the touch. Remember to top up the water if necessary. Remove the pudding from the saucepan and leave to rest for 5 minutes, before turning out on to a serving plate. Discard the small circle of baking parchment, then sprinkle with the chopped toasted hazelnuts. Keep warm.

Meanwhile, make the sauce. Place the butter, sugar and chocolate in a saucepan and heat until the chocolate has melted. Stir in the cream and simmer for 3 minutes until thickened. Pour over the pudding and serve.

Try This: FOR AN ALTERNATIVE: 344 FOR A MAIN MEAL: 254

Individual Steamed Chocolate Puddings

SERVES 8

150 g/5 oz unsalted butter, softened
175 g/6 oz light muscovado sugar
½ tsp freshly grated nutmeg
25 g/1 oz plain white flour,

sifted
4 tbsp cocoa powder, sifted
5 medium eggs, separated
125 g/4 oz ground almonds
50 g/2 oz fresh white breadcrumbs

To serve:
Greek yogurt
orange-flavoured chocolate curls

Preheat the oven to 180°C/350°F/Gas Mark 4, 10 minutes before baking. Lightly oil and line the bases of 8 individual 175 ml/6 fl oz pudding basins with a small circle of nonstick baking parchment. Cream the butter with 50 g/2 oz of the sugar and the nutmeg until light and fluffy.

Sift the flour and cocoa powder together, then stir into the creamed mixture. Beat in the egg yolks and mix well, then fold in the ground almonds and the breadcrumbs.

Whisk the egg whites in a clean grease-free bowl until stiff and standing in peaks then gradually whisk in the remaining sugar. Using a metal spoon, fold a quarter of the egg whites into the chocolate mixture and mix well, then fold in the remaining egg whites.

Spoon the mixture into the prepared basins, filling them two-thirds full to allow for expansion. Cover with a double sheet of tinfoil and secure tightly with string. Stand the pudding basins in a roasting tin and pour in sufficient water to come halfway up the sides of the basins.

Bake in the centre of the preheated oven for 30 minutes, or until the puddings are firm to the touch. Remove from the oven, loosen around the edges and invert onto warmed serving plates. Serve immediately with Greek yogurt and chocolate curls.

Try This: FOR AN ALTERNATIVE: 340   FOR A MAIN MEAL: 182

Chocolate Pear Pudding

SERVES 6

140 g/4½ oz butter, softened
2 tbsp soft brown sugar
400 g can of pear halves,
    drained and juice reserved
25 g/1 oz walnut halves

125 g/4 oz golden caster
    sugar
2 medium eggs, beaten
75 g/3 oz self-raising flour,
    sifted

50 g/2 oz cocoa powder
1 tsp baking powder
prepared chocolate custard
    (see p 340), to serve

Preheat the oven to 190°C/375°F/Gas Mark 5, 10 minutes before baking. Butter a 20.5 cm/8 inch sandwich tin with 15 g/½ oz of the butter and sprinkle the base with the soft brown sugar. Arrange the drained pear halves on top of the sugar, cut-side down. Fill the spaces between the pears with the walnut halves, flat-side upwards.

Cream the remaining butter with the caster sugar then gradually beat in the beaten eggs, adding 1 tablespoon of the flour after each addition. When all the eggs have been added, stir in the remaining flour.

Sift the cocoa powder and baking powder together, then stir into the creamed mixture with 1–2 tablespoons of the reserved pear juice to give a smooth dropping consistency.

Spoon the mixture over the pear halves, smoothing the surface. Bake in the preheated oven for 20–25 minutes, or until well risen and the surface springs back when lightly pressed.

Remove from the oven and leave to cool for 5 minutes. Using a palate knife, loosen the sides and invert onto a serving plate. Serve with custard.

Try This: FOR AN ALTERNATIVE: 378   FOR A MAIN MEAL: 212

Sticky Chocolate Surprise Pudding

SERVES 6–8

150 g/5 oz self-raising flour
25 g/1 oz cocoa powder
200 g/7 oz golden caster sugar
75 g/3 oz mint-flavoured
  chocolate, chopped
175 ml/6 fl oz full cream milk

2 tsp vanilla essence
50 g/2 oz unsalted butter,
  melted
1 medium egg
sprig of fresh mint, to
  decorate

For the sauce
175 g/6 oz dark muscovado
  sugar
125 g/4 oz cocoa powder
600 ml/1 pint very hot water

Preheat the oven to 180°C/350°F/Gas Mark 4, 10 minutes before baking. Lightly oil a 1.4 litre/2½ pint ovenproof soufflé dish. Sift the flour and cocoa powder into a large bowl and stir in the caster sugar and the chopped mint-flavoured chocolate and make a well in the centre.

Whisk the milk, vanilla essence and the melted butter together, then beat in the egg. Pour into the well in the dry ingredients and gradually mix together, drawing the dry ingredients in from the sides of the bowl. Beat well until mixed thoroughly. Spoon into the prepared soufflé dish.

To make the sauce, blend the dark muscovado sugar and the cocoa powder together and spoon over the top of the pudding. Carefully pour the hot water over the top of the pudding, but do not mix.

Bake in the preheated oven for 35–40 minutes, or until firm to the touch and the mixture has formed a sauce underneath. Decorate with mint and serve immediately.

Try This: FOR AN ALTERNATIVE: 332 FOR A MAIN MEAL: 178

Steamed
Chocolate Chip Pudding

SERVES 6

175 g/6 oz self-raising flour
½ tsp baking powder
75 g/3 oz fresh white
  breadcrumbs
125 g/4 oz shredded suet
125 g/4 oz golden caster
  sugar

2 medium eggs, lightly
  beaten
1 tsp vanilla essence
125 g/4 oz chocolate chips
150 ml/¼ pint cold milk
grated chocolate, to decorate

For the chocolate custard:
300 ml/½ pint milk
1 tbsp cornflour
1 tbsp cocoa powder
1 tbsp caster sugar
½ tsp vanilla essence
1 medium egg yolk

Lightly oil a 1.1 litre/2 pint pudding basin and line the base with a small circle of nonstick baking parchment.

Sift the flour and baking powder into a bowl, add the breadcrumbs, suet and sugar and mix well. Stir in the eggs and vanilla essence with the chocolate chips and mix with sufficient cold milk to form a smooth dropping consistency.

Spoon the mixture into the prepared basin and cover the pudding with a double sheet of baking parchment and then either a double sheet of tinfoil or a pudding cloth, with a pleat in the centre to allow for expansion. Secure tightly with string. Place in the top of a steamer, set over a saucepan of simmering water and steam for 1½–2 hours, or until the pudding is cooked and firm to the touch – replenish the water as necessary. Remove and leave to rest for 5 minutes before turning out onto a warmed serving plate.

Meanwhile, make the custard. Blend a little of the milk with the cornflour and cocoa powder to form a paste. Stir in the remaining milk with the sugar and vanilla essence. Pour into a saucepan and bring to the boil, stirring. Whisk in the egg yolk and cook for 1 minute. Decorate the pudding with grated chocolate and serve with the sauce.

Try This: FOR AN ALTERNATIVE: 334 FOR A MAIN MEAL: 112

White Chocolate Trifle

SERVES 6

1 homemade or bought
   chocolate Swiss roll,
   sliced
4 tbsp brandy
2 tbsp Irish cream liqueur
425 g can black cherries,
   drained and pitted, with

3 tbsp of the juice reserved
900 ml/1½ pints double
   cream
125 g/4 oz white chocolate,
   broken into pieces
6 medium egg yolks
50 g/2 oz caster sugar

2 tsp cornflour
1 tsp vanilla essence
50 g/2 oz plain dark
   chocolate, grated
50 g/2 oz milk chocolate,
   grated

Place the Swiss roll slices in the bottom of a trifle dish and pour over the brandy, Irish cream liqueur and a little of the reserved black cherry juice to moisten the Swiss roll. Arrange the black cherries on the top.

Pour 600 ml/1 pint of the cream into a saucepan and add the white chocolate. Heat gently to just below simmering point. Whisk together the egg yolks, caster sugar, cornflour and vanilla essence in a small bowl.

Gradually whisk the egg mixture into the hot cream, then strain into a clean saucepan and return to the heat.

Cook the custard gently, stirring throughout until thick and coats the back of a spoon.

Leave the custard to cool slightly, then pour over the trifle. Leave the trifle to chill in the refrigerator for at least 3–4 hours, or preferably overnight.

Before serving, lightly whip the remaining cream until soft peaks form, then spoon the cream over the set custard. Using the back of a spoon, swirl the cream in a decorative pattern. Sprinkle with grated plain and milk chocolate and serve.

Try This: FOR AN ALTERNATIVE: 318   FOR A MAIN MEAL: 212

Fruity Chocolate
Pudding with Sticky Chocolate Sauce

SERVES 4

125 g/4 oz muscovado sugar
1 orange, peeled and
   segmented
75 g/3 oz cranberries, fresh
   or thawed if frozen
125g/4 oz soft margarine
2 medium eggs
75 g/3 oz plain flour

½ tsp baking powder
3 tbsp cocoa powder
chocolate curls, to decorate

For the chocolate sauce:
175 g/6 oz plain dark
   chocolate, broken into
   pieces

50 g/2 oz butter
50 g/2 oz caster sugar
2 tbsp golden syrup
200 ml/7 fl oz milk

Lightly oil 4 x 200 ml 7 fl oz individual pudding basins and sprinkle with a little of the muscovado sugar. Place a few orange segments in each basin followed by a spoonful of the cranberries.

Cream the remaining muscovado sugar with the margarine until light and fluffy, then gradually beat in the eggs a little at a time, adding 1 tablespoon of the flour after each addition. Sift the remaining flour, baking powder and cocoa powder together, then stir into the creamed mixture with 1 tablespoon of cooled boiled water to give a soft dropping consistency. Spoon into the basins.

Cover each pudding with a double sheet of nonstick baking parchment with a pleat in the centre and secure tightly with string. Cover with a double sheet of tinfoil with a pleat in the centre to allow for expansion and secure tightly with string. Place in the top of a steamer, set over a saucepan of gently simmering water and steam steadily for 45 minutes, or until firm to the touch. Remember to replenish the water if necessary. Remove the puddings from the steamer and leave to rest for about 5 minutes before running a knife around the edges and turning out onto plates.

Meanwhile, make the chocolate sauce. Melt the chocolate and butter in a heatproof bowl set over a saucepan of gently simmering water. Add the sugar and golden syrup and stir until dissolved, then stir in the milk and continue to cook, stirring often, until the sauce thickens. Decorate the puddings with a few chocolate curls and serve with the sauce.

Try This: FOR AN ALTERNATIVE: 348   FOR A MAIN MEAL: 64

Chocolate Brioche Bake

SERVES 6

200 g/7 oz plain dark chocolate, broken into pieces
75 g/3 oz unsalted butter
225 g/8 oz brioche, sliced

1 tsp pure orange oil or 1 tbsp grated orange rind
½ tsp freshly grated nutmeg
3 medium eggs, beaten
25 g/1 oz golden caster sugar

600 ml/1 pint milk
cocoa powder and icing sugar for dusting

Preheat the oven to 180°C/350°F/Gas Mark 4, 10 minutes before baking. Lightly oil or butter a 1.7 litre/3 pint ovenproof dish. Melt the chocolate with 25 g/1 oz of the butter in a heatproof bowl set over a saucepan of simmering water. Stir until smooth.

Arrange half of the sliced brioche in the ovenproof dish, overlapping the slices slightly, then pour over half of the melted chocolate. Repeat the layers, finishing with a layer of chocolate.

Melt the remaining butter in a saucepan. Remove from the heat and stir in the orange oil or rind, the nutmeg and the beaten eggs. Continuing to stir, add the sugar and finally the milk. Beat thoroughly and pour over the brioche. Leave to stand for 30 minutes before baking.

Bake on the centre shelf in the preheated oven for 45 minutes, or until the custard is set and the topping is golden brown. Leave to stand for 5 minutes, then dust with cocoa powder and icing sugar. Serve warm.

Try This: FOR AN ALTERNATIVE: 330   FOR A MAIN MEAL: 252

Peach & Chocolate Bake

SERVES 6

200 g/7 oz plain dark
   chocolate
125 g/4 oz unsalted butter
4 medium eggs, separated

125 g/4 oz caster sugar
425 g can peach slices,
   drained
½ tsp ground cinnamon

1 tbsp icing sugar, sifted, to
   decorate
crème fraîche, to serve

Preheat the oven to 170°C/325°F/Gas Mark 3, 10 minutes before baking. Lightly oil a 1.7 litre/3 pint ovenproof dish.

Break the chocolate and butter into small pieces and place in a small heatproof bowl set over a saucepan of gently simmering water. Ensure the water is not touching the base of the bowl and leave to melt. Remove the bowl from the heat and stir until smooth.

Whisk the egg yolks with the sugar until very thick and creamy, then stir the melted chocolate and butter into the whisked egg yolk mixture and mix together lightly.

Place the egg whites in a clean grease-free bowl and whisk until stiff, then fold 2 tablespoons of the whisked egg whites into the chocolate mixture. Mix well, then add the remaining egg white and fold in very lightly.

Fold the peach slices and the cinnamon into the mixture, then spoon the mixture into the prepared dish. Do not level the mixture, leave a little uneven.

Bake in the preheated oven for 35–40 minutes, or until well risen and just firm to the touch. Sprinkle the bake with the icing sugar and serve immediately with spoonfuls of crème fraîche.

Try This: FOR AN ALTERNATIVE: 344   FOR A MAIN MEAL: 166

Black Forest Gateau

CUTS 10–12 SLICES

250 g/9 oz butter
1 tbsp instant coffee granules
350 ml/12 fl oz hot water
200 g/7 oz plain dark
   chocolate, chopped or
   broken

400 g/14 oz caster sugar
225 g/8 oz self-raising flour
150 g/5 oz plain flour
50 g/2 oz cocoa powder
2 medium eggs
2 tsp vanilla essence

2 x 400 g cans stoned
   cherries in juice
2 tsp arrowroot
600 ml/1 pint double cream
50 ml/2 fl oz kirsch

Preheat the oven to 150°C/300°F/Gas Mark 2, 5 minutes before serving. Lightly oil and line a deep 23 cm/9 inch cake tin.

Melt the butter in a large saucepan. Blend the coffee with the hot water, add to the butter with the chocolate and sugar and heat gently, stirring until smooth. Pour into a large bowl and leave until just warm. Sift together the flours and cocoa powder. Using an electric mixer, whisk the warm chocolate mixture on a low speed, then gradually whisk in the dry ingredients. Whisk in the eggs 1 at a time, then the vanilla essence. Pour the mixture into the prepared tin and bake in the preheated oven for 1 hour 45 minutes or until firm and a skewer inserted into the centre comes out clean. Leave in the tin for 5 minutes to cool slightly before turning out onto a wire rack.

Place the cherries and their juice in a small saucepan and heat gently. Blend the arrowroot with 2 teaspoons of water until smooth, then stir into the cherries. Cook, stirring, until the liquid thickens. Simmer very gently for 2 minutes, then leave until cold.

Whisk the double cream until thick. Trim the top of the cake if necessary, then split the cake into 3 layers. Brush the base of the cake with half the kirsch. Top with a layer of cream and one-third of the cherries. Repeat the layering, then place the third layer on top. Reserve a little cream for decorating and use the remainder to cover the top and sides of the cake. Pipe a decorative edge around the cake, then arrange the remaining cherries in the centre and serve.

Try This: FOR AN ALTERNATIVE: 352 FOR A MAIN MEAL: 292

Tiramisu

SERVES 4

225 g/8 oz mascarpone
  cheese
25 g/1 oz icing sugar, sifted
150 ml/¼ pint strong brewed
  coffee, chilled

300 ml/½ pint double cream
3 tbsp coffee liqueur
125 g/4 oz Savoiardi or
  sponge finger biscuits
50 g/2 oz plain dark

chocolate, grated or made
  into small curls
cocoa powder, for dusting
assorted summer berries, to
  serve

Lightly oil and line a 900 g/2 lb loaf tin with a piece of clingfilm. Put the mascarpone cheese and icing sugar into a large bowl and using a rubber spatula, beat until smooth. Stir in 2 tablespoons of chilled coffee and mix thoroughly.

Whip the cream with 1 tablespoon of the coffee liqueur until just thickened. Stir a spoonful of the whipped cream into the mascarpone mixture, then fold in the rest. Spoon half of the the mascarpone mixture into the prepared loaf tin and smooth the top.

Put the remaining coffee and coffee liqueur into a shallow dish just bigger than the biscuits. Using half of the biscuits, dip one side of each biscuit into the coffee mixture, then arrange on top of the mascarpone mixture in a single layer. Spoon the rest of the mascarpone mixture over the biscuits and smooth the top.

Dip the remaining biscuits in the coffee mixture and arrange on top of the mascarpone mixture. Drizzle with any remaining coffee mixture. Cover with clingfilm and chill in the refrigerator for 4 hours.

Carefully turn the tiramisu out on to a large serving plate and sprinkle with the grated chocolate or chocolate curls. Dust with cocoa powder, cut into slices and serve with a few summer berries.

Try This: FOR AN ALTERNATIVE: 350 FOR A MAIN MEAL: 128

Strawberry Flan

SERVES 4

For the sweet pastry:
175 g/6 oz plain flour
50 g/2 oz butter
50 g/2 oz white vegetable fat
2 tsp caster sugar
1 medium egg yolk, beaten

For the filling:
1 medium egg, plus 1 extra
  egg yolk
50 g/2 oz caster sugar
25 g/1 oz plain flour
300 ml/½ pint milk

few drops of vanilla essence
450 g/1 lb strawberries,
  cleaned and hulled
mint leaves, to decorate

Preheat the oven to 200°C/400°F/Gas Mark 6. Place the flour, butter and vegetable fat in a food processor and blend until the mixture resembles fine breadcrumbs. Stir in the sugar, then with the machine running, add the egg yolk and enough water to make a fairly stiff dough. Knead lightly, cover and chill in the refrigerator for 30 minutes.

Roll out the pastry and use to line a 23 cm/9 inch loose-bottomed flan tin. Place a piece of greaseproof paper in the pastry case and cover with baking beans or rice. Bake in the preheated oven for 15–20 minutes, until just firm. Reserve until cool.

Make the filling by whisking the eggs and sugar together until thick and pale. Gradually stir in the flour and then the milk. Pour into a small saucepan and simmer for 3–4 minutes stirring throughout.

Add the vanilla essence to taste, then pour into a bowl and leave to cool. Cover with greaseproof paper to prevent a skin from forming.

When the filling is cold, whisk until smooth then pour on to the cooked flan case. Slice the strawberries and arrange on the top of the filling. Decorate with the mint leaves and serve.

Try This: FOR AN ALTERNATIVE: 328   FOR A MAIN MEAL: 146

Raspberry & Almond Tart

SERVES 6–8

For the pastry:
225 g/8 oz plain flour
pinch of salt
125 g/4 oz butter, cut into
    pieces
50 g/2 oz caster sugar
grated zest of ½ lemon

1 medium egg yolk

For the filling:
75 g/3 oz butter
75 g/3 oz caster sugar
75 g/3 oz ground almonds
2 medium eggs

225 g/8 oz raspberries,
    thawed if frozen
2 tbsp slivered or flaked
    almonds
icing sugar for dusting

Preheat oven to 200°C/400°F/Gas Mark 6, 15 minutes before cooking. Blend the flour, salt and butter in a food processor until the mixture resembles breadcrumbs. Add the sugar and lemon zest and blend again for 1 minute. Mix the egg yolk with 2 tablespoons of cold water and add to the mixture. Blend until the mixture starts to come together, adding a little more water if necessary, then tip out on to a lightly floured surface. Knead until smooth, wrap in clingfilm and chill in the refrigerator for 30 minutes.

Roll the dough out thinly on a lightly floured surface and use to line a 23 cm/9 inch fluted tart tin. Chill in the refrigerator for 10 minutes. Line the pastry case with greaseproof paper and baking beans. Bake for 10 minutes, then remove the paper and beans and return to the oven for a further 10–12 minutes until cooked. Allow to cool slightly, then reduce the oven temperature to 190°C/ 375°F/Gas Mark 5.

Blend together the butter, sugar, ground almonds, and eggs until smooth. Spread the raspberries over the base of the pastry, then cover with the almond mixture. Bake for 15 minutes. Remove from the oven and sprinkle with the slivered or flaked almonds and dust generously with icing sugar. Bake for a further 15–20 minutes, until firm and golden brown. Leave to cool, then serve.

Try This: FOR AN ALTERNATIVE: 362   FOR A MAIN MEAL: 178

Rich Double-crust Plum Pie

SERVES 6

For the pastry:
75 g/3 oz butter
75 g/3 oz white vegetable fat
225 g/8 oz plain flour

2 medium egg yolks

For the filling:
450 g/1 lb fresh plums,

preferably Victoria
50 g/2 oz caster sugar
1 tbsp milk
a little extra caster sugar

Preheat the oven to 200°C/400°F/Gas Mark 6. Make the pastry by rubbing the butter and white vegetable fat into the flour until it resembles fine breadcrumbs or blend in a food processor. Add the egg yolks and enough water to make a soft dough. Knead lightly, then wrap and leave in the refrigerator for about 30 minutes.

Meanwhile, prepare the fruit. Rinse and dry the plums, then cut in half and remove the stones. Slice the plums into chunks and cook in a saucepan with 25 g/1 oz of the sugar and 2 tablespoons of water for 5–7 minutes, or until slightly softened. Remove from the heat and add the remaining sugar to taste and allow to cool.

Roll out half the chilled pastry on a lightly floured surface and use to line the base and sides of a 1.1 litre/ 2 pint pie dish. Allow the pastry to hang over the edge of the dish. Spoon in the prepared plums.

Roll out the remaining pastry to use as the lid and brush the edge with a little water. Wrap the pastry around the rolling pin and place over the plums. Press the edges together to seal and mark a decorative edge around the rim of the pastry by pinching with the thumb and forefinger or using the back of a fork. Brush the lid with milk, and make a few slits in the top. Use any trimmings to decorate the top of the pie with pastry leaves. Place on a baking sheet and bake in the preheated oven for 30 minutes, or until golden brown. Sprinkle with a little caster sugar and serve hot or cold.

Try This: FOR AN ALTERNATIVE: 354   FOR A MAIN MEAL: 210

Egg Custard Tart

SERVES 6

For the sweet pastry:
50 g/2 oz butter
50 g/2 oz white vegetable fat
175 g/6 oz plain flour
1 medium egg yolk, beaten

2 tsp caster sugar

For the filling:
300 ml/½ pint milk
2 medium eggs, plus

1 medium egg yolk
25 g/1 oz caster sugar
½ tsp freshly grated nutmeg

Preheat the oven to 200°C/400°F/Gas Mark 6. Oil a 20.5 cm/8 inch flan tin or dish.

Make the pastry by cutting the butter and vegetable fat into small cubes. Add to the flour in a large bowl and rub in, until the mixture resembles fine breadcrumbs. Add the egg, sugar and enough water to form a soft and pliable dough. Turn on to a lightly floured board and knead. Wrap and chill in the refrigerator for 30 minutes.

Roll the pastry out on to a lightly floured surface or pastry board and use to line the oiled flan tin. Place in the refrigerator to reserve.

Warm the milk in a small saucepan. Briskly whisk together the eggs, egg yolk and caster sugar. Pour the milk into the egg mixture and whisk until blended. Strain through a sieve into the pastry case. Place the flan tin on a baking sheet.

Sprinkle the top of the tart with nutmeg and bake in the preheated oven for about 15 minutes.

Turn the oven down to 170°C/325°F/Gas Mark 3 and bake for a further 30 minutes, or until the custard has set. Serve hot or cold.

Try This: FOR AN ALTERNATIVE: 366   FOR A MAIN MEAL: 262

Iced Bakewell Tart

CUTS INTO 8 SLICES

For the rich pastry:
175 g/6 oz plain flour
pinch of salt
60 g/2½ oz butter, cut into
    small pieces
50 g/2 oz white vegetable
    fat, cut into small pieces
2 small egg yolks, beaten

For the filling:
125 g/4 oz butter, melted
125 g/4 oz caster sugar
125 g/4 oz ground almonds
2 large eggs, beaten
few drops of almond
    essence
2 tbsp seedless raspberry jam

For the icing:
125 g/4 oz icing sugar, sifted
6–8 tsp fresh lemon juice
25 g/1 oz toasted flaked
    almonds

Preheat the oven to 200°C/400°F/Gas Mark 6. Place the flour and salt in a bowl, rub in the butter and vegetable fat until the mixture resembles breadcrumbs. Alternatively, blend quickly, in short bursts in a food processor.

Add the eggs with sufficient water to make a soft, pliable dough. Knead lightly on a floured board then chill in the refrigerator for about 30 minutes. Roll out the pastry and use to line a 23 cm/9 inch loose-bottomed flan tin.

For the filling, mix together the melted butter, sugar, almonds and beaten eggs and add a few drops of almond essence. Spread the base of the pastry case with the raspberry jam and spoon over the egg mixture. Bake in the preheated oven for about 30 minutes, or until the filling is firm and golden brown. Remove from the oven and allow to cool completely.

When the tart is cold make the icing by mixing together the icing sugar and lemon juice, a little at a time, until the icing is smooth and of a spreadable consistency.

Spread the icing over the tart, leave to set for 2–3 minutes and sprinkle with the almonds. Chill in the refrigerator for about 10 minutes and serve.

Try This: FOR AN ALTERNATIVE: 356   FOR A MAIN MEAL: 118

Almond & Pine Nut Tart

SERVES 6

250 g/9 oz ready-made
    sweet shortcrust pastry
75 g/3 oz blanched almonds
75 g/3 oz caster sugar
pinch of salt
2 medium eggs

1 tsp vanilla essence
2–3 drops almond essence
125 g/4 oz unsalted butter,
    softened
2 tbsp flour
½ tsp baking powder

3–4 tbsp raspberry jam
50 g/2 oz pine nuts
icing sugar, to decorate
whipped cream, to serve

Preheat oven to 200°C/400°F/Gas Mark 6. Roll out the pastry and use to line a 23 cm/9 inch fluted flan tin. Chill in the refrigerator for 10 minutes, then line with greaseproof paper and baking beans and bake blind in the preheated oven for 10 minutes. Remove the paper and beans and bake for a further 10–12 minutes until cooked. Leave to cool. Reduce the temperature to 190°C/375°F/Gas Mark 5.

Grind the almonds in a food processor until fine. Add the sugar, salt, eggs, vanilla and almond essence and blend. Add the butter, flour and baking powder and blend until smooth.

Spread a thick layer of the raspberry jam over the cooled pastry case, then pour in the almond filling. Sprinkle the pine nuts evenly over the top and bake for 30 minutes, until firm and browned.

Remove the tart from the oven and leave to cool. Dust generously with icing sugar and serve cut into wedges with whipped cream.

Try This: FOR AN ALTERNATIVE: 362   FOR A MAIN MEAL: 242

Goats' Cheese & Lemon Tart

SERVES 8–10

For the pastry:
125 g/4 oz butter, cut into
    small pieces
225 g/8 oz plain flour
pinch of salt
50 g/2 oz caster sugar

1 medium egg yolk

For the filling:
350 g/12 oz mild fresh goats'
    cheese, eg Chavroux
3 medium eggs, beaten

150 g/5 oz caster sugar
grated rind and juice of 3
    lemons
450 ml/¾ pint double cream
fresh raspberries, to
    decorate and serve

Preheat oven to 200˚C/400˚F/Gas Mark 6, 15 minutes before cooking. Rub the butter into the plain flour and salt until the mixture resembles breadcrumbs, then stir in the sugar. Beat the egg yolk with 2 tablespoons of cold water and add to the mixture. Mix together until a dough is formed then turn the dough out on to a lightly floured surface and knead until smooth. Chill in the refrigerator for 30 minutes.

Roll the dough out thinly on a lightly floured surface and use to line a 4 cm/1½ inch deep 23 cm/9 inch fluted flan tin. Chill in the refrigerator for 10 minutes. Line the pastry case with greaseproof paper and baking beans or tinfoil and bake blind in the preheated oven for 10 minutes. Remove the paper and beans or tinfoil. Return to the oven for a further 12–15 minutes until cooked. Leave to cool slightly, then reduce the oven temperature to 150˚C/300˚F/Gas Mark 2.

Beat the goats' cheese until smooth. Whisk in the eggs, sugar, lemon rind and juice. Add the cream and mix well.

Carefully pour the cheese mixture into the pastry case and return to the oven. Bake in the oven for 35–40 minutes, or until just set. If it begins to brown or swell, open the oven door for 2 minutes, then reduce the temperature to 120˚C/250˚F/Gas Mark ½ and leave the tart to cool in the oven. Chill in the refrigerator until cold. Decorate and serve with fresh raspberries.

Try This: FOR AN ALTERNATIVE: 372   FOR A MAIN MEAL: 114

Frozen Mississippi Mud Pie

CUTS 6–8 SLICES

1 quantity Ginger Crumb
  Crust (see page 380)
600 ml/1 pint chocolate ice
  cream
600 ml/1 pint coffee-
flavoured ice cream

For the chocolate topping:
175 g/6 oz plain dark
  chocolate, chopped

50 ml/2 fl oz single cream
1 tbsp golden syrup
1 tsp vanilla essence
50 g/2 oz coarsely grated
  white and milk chocolate

Prepare the crumb crust and use to line a 23 cm/9 inch loose-based flan tin and freeze for 30 minutes.

Soften the ice creams at room temperature for about 25 minutes. Spoon the chocolate ice cream into the crumb crust, spreading it evenly over the base, then spoon the coffee ice cream over the chocolate ice cream, mounding it slightly in the centre. Return to the freezer to refreeze the ice cream.

For the topping, heat the dark chocolate with the cream, golden syrup and vanilla essence in a saucepan. Stir until the chocolate has melted and is smooth. Pour into a bowl and chill in the refrigerator, stirring occasionally, until cold but not set.

Spread the cooled chocolate mixture over the top of the frozen pie. Sprinkle with the chocolate and return to the freezer for 1½ hours or until firm. Serve at room temperature.

Try This: FOR AN ALTERNATIVE: 370 FOR A MAIN MEAL: 208

Mocha Pie

SERVES 4–6

1 x 23 cm/9 inch ready-made sweet pastry case

For the filling:
125 g/4 oz plain dark chocolate, broken into pieces

175 g/6 oz unsalted butter
225 g/8 oz soft brown sugar
1 tsp vanilla essence
3 tbsp strong black coffee

For the topping:
600 ml/1 pint double cream

50 g/2 oz icing sugar
2 tsp vanilla essence
1 tsp instant coffee dissolved in 1 tsp boiling water and cooled
grated plain and white chocolate, to decorate

Place the prepared pastry case on a large serving plate and reserve. Melt the chocolate in a heatproof bowl set over a saucepan of simmering water. Ensure the water is not touching the base of the bowl. Remove from the heat, stir until smooth and leave to cool.

Cream the butter, soft brown sugar and vanilla essence until light and fluffy, then beat in the cooled chocolate. Add the strong black coffee, pour into the pastry case and chill in the refrigerator for about 30 minutes.

For the topping, whisk the cream until beginning to thicken, then whisk in the sugar and vanilla essence. Continue to whisk until the cream is softly peaking. Spoon just under half of the cream into a separate bowl and fold in the dissolved coffee.

Spread the remaining cream over the filling in the pastry case. Spoon the coffee-flavoured whipped cream evenly over the top, then swirl it decoratively with a palate knife. Sprinkle with grated chocolate and chill in the refrigerator until ready to serve.

Try This: FOR AN ALTERNATIVE: 368   FOR A MAIN MEAL: 200

Triple
Chocolate Cheesecake

SERVES 6

For the base:
150 g/5 oz digestive biscuits, crushed
50 g/2 oz butter, melted

For the cheesecake:
75 g/3 oz white chocolate,
roughly chopped
300 ml/½ pint double cream
50 g/2 oz caster sugar
3 medium eggs, beaten
400 g/14 oz full fat soft cream cheese
2 tbsp cornflour

75 g/3 oz plain dark chocolate, roughly chopped
75 g/3 oz milk chocolate, roughly chopped
fromage frais, to serve

Preheat the oven to 180°C/350°F/Gas Mark 4, 10 minutes before baking. Lightly oil a 23 x 7.5 cm/9 x 3 inch springform tin.

To make the base, mix together the crushed biscuits and melted butter. Press into the base of the tin and leave to set. Chill in the refrigerator.

Place the white chocolate and cream in a small heavy-based saucepan and heat gently until the chocolate has melted. Stir until smooth and reserve.

Beat the sugar and eggs together until light and creamy in colour, add the cream cheese and beat until the mixture is smooth and free from lumps. Stir the reserved white chocolate cream together with the cornflour into the soft cream cheese mixture.

Add the dark and milk chocolate to the soft cream cheese mixture and mix lightly together until blended. Spoon over the chilled base, place on a baking sheet and bake in the preheated oven for 1 hour.

Switch off the heat, open the oven door and leave the cheesecake to cool in the oven. Chill in the refrigerator for at least 6 hours before removing the cheesecake from the tin. Cut into slices and transfer to serving plates. Serve with fromage frais.

Try This: FOR AN ALTERNATIVE: 366 FOR A MAIN MEAL: 220

Chocolate Mallow Pie

SERVES 6

200 g/7 oz digestive biscuits	chocolate	300 ml/½ pint double cream
75 g/3 oz butter, melted	20 marshmallows	
175 g/6 oz plain dark	1 medium egg, separated	

Place the biscuits in a polythene bag and finely crush with a rolling pin. Alternatively, place in a food processor and blend until fine crumbs are formed.

Melt the butter in a medium-sized sauce-pan, add the crushed biscuits and mix together. Press into the base of the prepared tin and leave to cool in the refrigerator.

Melt 125 g/4 oz of the chocolate with the marshmallows and 2 tablespoons of water in a saucepan over a gentle heat, stirring constantly. Leave to cool slightly, then stir in the egg yolk, beat well, then return to the refrigerator until cool.

Whisk the egg white until stiff and standing in peaks, then fold into the chocolate mixture.

Lightly whip the cream and fold three-quarters of the cream into the chocolate mixture. Reserve the remainder. Spoon the chocolate cream into the flan case and chill in the refrigerator until set.

When ready to serve, spoon the remaining cream over the chocolate pie, swirling in a decorative pattern. Grate the remaining dark chocolate and sprinkle over the cream, then serve.

Try This: FOR AN ALTERNATIVE: 380   FOR A MAIN MEAL: 156

Chocolate Pecan Pie

CUTS INTO 8–10 SLICES

225 g/8 oz prepared
shortcrust pastry
200 g/7 oz pecan halves
125 g/4 oz plain dark

chocolate, chopped
25 g/1 oz butter, diced
3 medium eggs
125 g/4 oz light brown sugar

175 ml/6 fl oz golden syrup
2 tsp vanilla essence
vanilla ice cream, to serve

Preheat the oven to 180°C/350°F/Gas Mark 4, 10 minutes before baking. Roll the prepared pastry out on a lightly floured surface and use to line a 25.5 cm/10 inch pie plate. Roll the trimmings out and use to make a decorative edge around the pie, then chill in the refrigerator for 1 hour.

Reserve about 60 perfect pecan halves, or enough to cover the top of the pie, then coarsely chop the remainder and reserve. Melt the chocolate and butter in a small saucepan over a low heat or in the microwave and reserve.

Beat the eggs and brush the base and sides of the pastry with a little of the beaten egg. Beat the sugar, golden syrup and vanilla essence into the beaten eggs. Add the pecans, then beat in the chocolate mixture.

Pour the filling into the pastry case and arrange the reserved pecan halves in concentric circles over the top. Bake in the preheated oven for 45–55 minutes, or until the filling is well risen and just set. If the pastry edge begins to brown too quickly, cover with strips of tinfoil. Remove from the oven and serve with ice cream.

Try This: FOR AN ALTERNATIVE: 364   FOR A MAIN MEAL: 196

Pear & Chocolate Custard Tart

CUTS INTO 6–8 SLICES

For the chocolate pastry:
125 g/4 oz unsalted butter, softened
60 g/2½ oz caster sugar
2 tsp vanilla essence
175 g/6 oz plain flour, sifted

40 g/1½ oz cocoa powder
whipped cream, to serve

For the filling:
125 g/4 oz plain dark chocolate, chopped

225 ml/8 fl oz whipping cream
50 g/2 oz caster sugar
1 large egg
1 large egg yolk
1 tbsp crème de cacao
3 ripe pears

Preheat the oven to 190°C/375°F/Gas Mark 5, 10 minutes before baking. To make the pastry, put the butter, sugar and vanilla essence into a food processor and blend until creamy. Add the flour and cocoa powder and process until a soft dough forms. Remove the dough, wrap in clingfilm and chill in the refrigerator for at least 1 hour. Roll out the dough between 2 sheets of clingfilm to a 28 cm/11 inch round. Peel off the top sheet of clingfilm and invert the pastry round into a lightly oiled 23 cm/9 inch loose-based flan tin, easing the dough into the base and sides. Prick the base with a fork, then chill in the refrigerator for 1 hour. Place a sheet of nonstick baking parchment and baking beans in the case and bake blind in the preheated oven for 10 minutes. Remove the parchment and beans and bake for a further 5 minutes. Remove and cool.

To make the filling, heat the chocolate, cream and half the sugar in a medium saucepan over a low heat, stirring until melted and smooth. Remove from the heat and cool slightly before beating in the egg, egg yolk and crème de cacao. Spread evenly over the pastry case base. Peel the pears, then cut each pear in half and carefully remove the core. Cut each half crossways into thin slices and arrange over the custard, gently fanning the slices towards the centre and pressing into the chocolate custard. Bake in the oven for 10 minutes. Reduce the oven temperature to 180°C/350°F/Gas Mark 4 and sprinkle the surface evenly with the remaining sugar. Bake in the oven for 20–25 minutes, or until the custard is set and the pears are tender and glazed. Remove from the oven and leave to cool slightly. Cut into slices, then serve with spoonfuls of whipped cream.

Try This: FOR AN ALTERNATIVE: 336 FOR A MAIN MEAL: 176

Double Chocolate Banoffee Tart

CUTS INTO 8 SLICES

2 x 400 g cans sweetened
   condensed milk
175 g/6 oz plain dark
   chocolate, chopped
600 ml/1 pint whipping cream
1 tbsp golden syrup

25 g/1 oz butter, diced
150 g/5 oz white chocolate,
   grated or finely chopped
1 tsp vanilla essence
2–3 ripe bananas
cocoa powder, for dusting

For the ginger crumb crust:
24–26 gingernut biscuits,
   roughly crushed
100 g/3½ oz butter, melted
1–2 tbsp sugar, or to taste
½ tsp ground ginger

Preheat the oven to 190°C/375°F/Gas Mark 5, 10 minutes before baking. Place the condensed milk in a heavy-based saucepan over a gentle heat. Bring to the boil, stirring constantly. Boil gently for about 3–5 minutes or until golden. Remove from the heat and leave to cool. To make the crust, place the biscuits with the melted butter, sugar and ginger in a food processor and blend together. Press into the sides and base of 23 cm/9 inch loose-based flan tin with the back of a spoon. Chill in the refrigerator for 15–20 minutes, then bake in the preheated oven for 5–6 minutes. Remove from the oven and leave to cool.

Melt the dark chocolate in a medium-sized saucepan with 150 ml/¼ pint of the whipping cream, the golden syrup and the butter over a low heat. Stir until smooth. Carefully pour into the crumb crust, tilting the tin to distribute the chocolate layer evenly. Chill in the refrigerator for at least 1 hour or until set.

Heat 150 ml/¼ pint of the remaining cream until hot, then add the white chocolate and stir until smooth. Stir in the vanilla essence and strain into a bowl. Leave to cool to room temperature. Scrape the cooked condensed milk into a bowl and whisk until smooth, adding a little of the remaining cream if too thick. Spread over the chocolate layer, then slice the bananas and arrange evenly over the top. Whisk the remaining cream until soft peaks form. Stir a spoonful of the cream into the white chocolate mixture, then fold in the remaining cream. Spread over the bananas, to the edge. Dust with cocoa powder and chill in the refrigerator until ready to serve.

Try This: FOR AN ALTERNATIVE: 374   FOR A MAIN MEAL: 228

Index